INSTANT GRATIFICATION

LAUREN CHATTMAN

WILLIAM MORROW
AN IMPRINT OF HARPERCOLLINSPUBLISHERS

NO-HASSLE DESSERTS

INSTANT

GRATIFICATION

IN JUST ABOUT NO TIME

FIRST EDITION

Designed by Marysarah Quinn

Printed on acid-free paper

Library of Congress Cataloging-in-Publication Data

Chattman, Lauren.
    Instant gratification : no-hassle desserts in just about no time /
by Lauren Chattman.—1st ed.
        p. cm.
    Includes index.
    ISBN 0-688-16910-4
    1. Desserts. 2. Quick and easy cookery. I. Title.
TX773 .C474 2000
641.8'6—dc21   99-053370

        00 01 02 03 04 /FF 10 9 8 7 6 5 4 3 2 1

FOR ROSE AND EVE

Acknowledgments

Thanks once again to Angela Miller for supporting this project from start to finish.

I'm lucky to have Pam Hoenig as my editor. This is my third book with Pam, and she's helped shape my ideas into a consistent take on simple home cooking.

Carrie Weinberg and Corinne Alhadeff continue to work so hard and with such terrific results on my behalf.

Marysarah Quinn's book designs have been just perfect.

Thanks to John Willoughby for his kind words and continuing support. Nick Malgieri has been an inspiration since I attended his professional pastry program at Peter Kump's New York Cooking School.

Yvette Willock provided invaluable baby-sitting services throughout the writing of this book.

Special thanks to Jack Bishop, who valiantly taste-tested and approved everything that appears here.

And thanks to Jack, Rose, and Eve for making every day so sweet.

Contents

Introduction

DESSERT EVERY DAY

As a child, I watched in awe at Thanksgiving time as my great-grandmother undertook the backbreaking task of making deep-dish apple pie for twenty. She mixed the dough by hand, rolled it into impossibly large and thin sheets, prepped mountains of apples. The pies took three days to complete. During breaks from her task, she would go to the freezer and raid her supply of miniature frozen Milky Way bars. She just couldn't work for days on a dessert, no matter how great it was destined to be, without getting a little bit of instant gratification during the process. Apple pie was an occasional treat; dessert was an everyday necessity.

Maybe it is genetic. I went to cooking school to learn how to make fancy bakery-style cakes. I spent long days toiling in restaurant kitchens to produce those labor-intensive desserts that people take for granted when they're not cooking for themselves. But at home I satisfied my sweet tooth on a daily basis with creamy chocolate pudding and buttery brown sugar cupcakes. Like my grandmother, I just couldn't wait for dessert.

Having written two books about quick and easy cooking, I knew that it was possible to make great meals with very little effort. My first book, *Cool Kitchen*, had over 100 recipes that required no cooking at all. *Just Add Water* was limited to recipes that required only one kitchen skill—boiling. After having so much fun and success with this food, I can tell you that I had very little incentive to return to hard kitchen labor. I wanted to try my luck with desserts. But could real desserts—I'm not talking about a dish of store-bought ice cream dressed up with a few berries, but cakes, cookies, and delicious fruit tarts—be had as simply and quickly?

I was expecting another baby, so it was the perfect time to put on a few extra pounds trying. After months of testing and tasting quick desserts, sometimes one a day, sometimes five or six, I am happy to report that there are many ways to make a great dessert in 15 minutes or less. In fact, I fell in love with so many of the things I made that I now spend more time deciding what to make for dessert than I do actually preparing it. It might take me an hour to choose between Chocolate-Buttermilk Snacking Cake, Oat-Crisped Pears with Sour Cream, or Honey and Almond Brittle. But whatever I choose, I know it won't take me more than 15 minutes to make. With a newborn and a preschooler demanding so much attention, that's probably all the time I'll have each day to put together something sweet. Knowing now how fabulous a 15-minute dessert can be, I wouldn't want to spend an extra minute, even if I had all the time in the world.

Having figured out how to surprise and delight my family and friends with wonderful sweets while expending as little effort as possible, it is my pleasure to share these desserts with you. It's like the pleasure some people get from telling everyone that they purchased their great-looking designer clothes for 60 percent off. Nothing gives me more joy than being able to honestly reply to my guests' exclamations that whatever they are eating was prepared in 15 minutes. If this kind of boasting thrills you too, keep reading.

DEFINING THE 15-MINUTE DESSERT

Early on, I set some goals and ground rules for *Instant Gratification*. I wanted the desserts to satisfy my desire for classic flavors (chocolate, almond, apple) and textures (crispy, creamy, juicy). I wanted each one to taste homemade, wholesome, and fresh; no boxed brownie mixes, Jell-O, or marshmallow fluff. I settled on 15 minutes maximum preparation time, excluding any baking time or cooling time since this would severely limit what I could make. I think this is fair, because when a dessert is in the oven or sitting on a wire rack, I can use the time to do other things, or nothing at all.

Soon after getting to work, I began to understand what would and wouldn't be possible in 15 minutes. Desserts with multiple components were out; so was anything that had to be shaped or decorated. Cakes would have to be unfilled and unfrosted, cookies would have to be dropped rather than rolled and cut.

But there was no limit to the variety of desserts I could produce. With a little bit of tinkering, I've figured out ways of producing candies, custards, crepes, and so much more in the allotted time. I was willing to try any promising flavor, ingredient, or technique. My ecumenical tastes led me to desserts highlighting unusual flavors or combinations, like Tea-Infused Panna Cotta and Sweet and Spicy Pecan Brittle. These desserts are not bizarre or outrageous, but utterly natural. A panna cotta flavored with tea is just as familiar and soothing as a cup of sweetened, milky Earl Grey. Nut brittle spiked with cayenne pepper is as addictive as a fistful of Red Hot Dollars. And there are plenty of comforting old favorites to satisfy purists and classicists—pecan pie, berry shortcakes, s'mores—updated for maximum speed and goodness.

A few guiding principles shaped the recipes:

Streamlined ingredients lists. One of the most time-consuming things about cooking is actually gathering together a long list of items. To save time, my recipes rely on just a few premium ingredients combined to showcase the flavors and textures that we crave when it comes to dessert. Ginger-Spiced Custards contains only milk, cream, ginger, eggs, and

sugar; the result is a silky dessert with a bit of a flavor edge. Bittersweet Chocolate Meringue Cookies, crispy on the outside and chewy on the inside, are made with just egg whites, sugar, cocoa powder, and miniature chocolate chips.

Carefully constructed recipes. My recipes are road maps with all the shortcuts spelled out. The recipe for Warm Gingerbread Squares outlines the most efficient way to put together this simple dessert—prepare the cake pan and bring some water to boil in a saucepan. Stir in the molasses and baking soda and remove from the heat. While this mixture is cooling, cream the butter and sugar in the food processor and add the egg yolk. Pour in the molasses mixture, pulse, add the dry ingredients, and pulse again. Scrape into the prepared pan and bake. Each recipe lists required equipment before the ingredients list (a 9-inch cake pan, nonstick cooking spray, a food processor or mixer, a rubber spatula) to help the cook get organized. The headnotes don't just rhapsodize about the recipes, but contain useful information, tips, and serving suggestions.

Innovative pastry techniques and substitutions. Classic pies, cakes, and tarts always take more than 15 minutes, because they consist of several separate components that have to be prepared separately. Instead of mixing, chilling, rolling, docking, and baking a traditional tart shell (not to mention making tricky pastry cream), I might press chocolate cookie crumbs, ground almonds, and butter into the bottom of a tart pan and fill the shell with sweetened mascarpone and fresh berries.

World cuisines and ingredients. Sometimes I'll come across a little-known recipe that nevertheless perfectly suits our dessert tastes now. Fresh Fig Mousse, inspired by a traditional recipe in Colman Andrews's *Catalan Cuisine*, is a sophisticated mixture of figs, walnuts, anisette, and cream that couldn't be quicker to prepare. A single unusual ingredient might inspire a casual but unusual dessert: wonton wrappers brushed with butter and sprinkled with sugar bake up in 4 minutes and combine with sliced plums and whipped cream to make quick "shortcakes."

HOW TO FIND
INSTANT GRATIFICATION

Sometimes you are in the mood for a certain kind of sweet (cookies, pudding, candy).

Sometimes you need something special to serve to dinner guests. Sometimes you just need something sweet *fast. Instant Gratification* is organized around these needs.

Chapter 1 is a collection of great desserts that are ready to eat in 15 minutes flat. Whether you are making dessert on the spur of the moment or you want something extra quick to end a casual meal for family or friends, this is the place to look.

For some people, nothing answers the hunger for dessert like a crisp pastry crust containing a fruity or creamy filling. Chapter 2 focuses on desserts that are easier than pie but satisfy just the same.

For the best simple cakes and cupcakes, turn to Chapter 3.

Comfort food is the focus of Chapter 4, with recipes for the simplest puddings, custards, and mousses.

Chapter 5 is for nibblers, with recipes for cookies and candy.

Desserts for company don't have to be time-consuming. Chapter 6 contains a marvelous collection of special sweets that are celebratory and festive without any fuss.

◆

ACCOMPLISHING THE 15-MINUTE DESSERT

Every time I tested a recipe, I set my kitchen timer for 15 minutes. Before actually beginning to cook, I methodically went through the equipment and ingredients lists preceding each recipe and got out everything I needed. Then I forced myself to work calmly and naturally, trying not to cram too much work in before my buzzer went off. You have my promise that I did not resemble a character in a speeded-up silent movie or a contestant on *Beat the Clock*. If I could not complete the recipe in the allotted time, I either rejected or reworked it.

Some of the recipes require some downtime, which I didn't count. When I used puff pastry, I put the rolled dough in the freezer for 15 minutes and stopped the clock. Neither did I count baking time, cooling time, or time that frozen desserts need to spend in the freezer before serving. Since I use this time to read to my daughter, make dinner, do some catalog shopping, or take a nap, I think this is fair.

Even very quick and simple recipes require more than the wave of a magic wand. To produce quality desserts quickly, you must be organized and work deliberately. Read the recipe carefully before you start to cook.

Gather your equipment and ingredients, making sure that you have everything you need before you start. The time you take to understand a recipe before you actually start cooking will be saved later when you can work purposefully rather than searching here and there for the missing bottle of vanilla or wire whisk.

5 MINUTES EXTRA

As I was developing these recipes, I was continually amazed at the quality of the desserts I could produce in 15 minutes. Such quick work left me with a lot of energy. What could I do with a particular dessert if I wanted to spend just a few more minutes on it? Mostly I was satisfied with what I already had. But occasionally I had an idea about how to gild the lily, and I have passed these along in little boxes at the end of certain recipes. Want to serve Pumpkin-Spice Pound Cake to company? Toast slices of cake and serve warm with Ginger Mascarpone. Love the combination of ginger and chocolate? Dip your Chewy Ginger-Molasses Cookies in some melted bittersweet chocolate.

Rather than leaving you exhausted, the recipes in this book should exhilarate and inspire you. After completing the preparations for desserts ranging from Olive Oil and Orange

Cake to Roasted Grapes with Soft-Ripened Blue Cheese in 15 minutes or less, you might want to rest on your laurels. But when you've got so much time to spare, you might come up with some ideas of your own for making an almost instant dessert even more gratifying.

EQUIPMENT FOR INSTANT GRATIFICATION

I wish I could report that all simple desserts can be conjured up with a mixing bowl and a wooden spoon. But the truth is, to save time, you have to have the right equipment. While there are many recipes in this book that can literally be stirred together, there are also some that depend on labor-saving tools. The good news is, only a couple of these items are expensive. An electric mixer and food processor are indispensable in blending batter, whipping cream, and beating egg whites. These machines are well worth the money if you love dessert but want to gain some independence from your local bakery. The rest of the stuff that I routinely use is pretty basic. If it's not already in your utility drawer, you can probably buy it for a few dollars in the baking aisle of your supermarket.

Baking pans: One 8-inch and one 9-inch round cake pan, an 8-inch square baking pan, and an 8 × 4-inch loaf pan will allow you to bake a wide variety of cakes. Loaf pans are also necessary for making molded frozen desserts like Frozen Lemon Sabayon Terrine with Kiwis and Raspberries. You'll need standard-size muffin tins and mini muffin tins for cupcakes.

Baking sheets: I like insulated baking sheets, which prevent cookies from scorching on the bottom before they are cooked through. They cost a little extra, and are available at cookware stores.

Double boiler: A double boiler is just a pot within a pot, used to heat delicate ingredients like eggs or chocolate over indirect heat. It is not necessary to buy a double boiler, since you can easily improvise one by placing a stainless steel bowl over a saucepan filled with an inch of simmering water.

Electric mixer with paddle and whisk attachments: My KitchenAid mixer stands proudly on my counter, ready for service at any time. With the paddle attachment, it makes quick work of creaming butter and sugar. With its wire whisk, it whips cream and beats egg whites to stiff peaks in seconds. Standing mixers and handheld mixers fitted only with beater attachments will do the same jobs, but might take a minute or two longer.

Food processor with metal blade: I use a food processor for everything from chopping nuts to pureeing strawberries. Even faster than an electric mixer, it can blend cake batter in seconds. Why not let it do all the work for you?

Knives: While you won't need an entire knife block full of cutlery, a large, heavy chef's knife and a small, sharp paring knife are often necessary for making quick desserts. High-quality knives are a real pleasure. Not only will they allow you to peel, chop, and slice faster than bad knives, but they are more comfortable to hold and make cooking a fun hobby instead of a difficult chore.

Measuring cups and spoons: While you can get away with "a little bit of this, a little bit of that" when throwing together a quick pasta sauce, eyeballing it just won't do for most desserts. Use clear "liquid" measuring cups for liquid ingredients, plastic or metal "dry" measuring cups for large quantities of dry ingredients, and measuring spoons for small

quantities. Fill cups and spoons completely and level off with a knife for precise measurements.

Mixing bowls: Not only are mixing bowls essential for mixing, they are great for organizing ingredients before you start to cook. I like to measure all my ingredients into small bowls before I actually begin to cook, so that actually putting together a dessert is just a matter of quickly combining a few parts. Sets of nesting glass and metal mixing bowls are inexpensive and can be purchased at any cookware shop.

Nonstick cooking spray: If you've ever experienced the agony of overturning a cake onto a wire rack only to see its bottom half stuck to the pan, you have probably already switched from butter to nonstick cooking spray. This is an item I cannot live without. Not only is cooking spray quicker than greasing a pan with butter, it is much more reliable.

Parchment paper: Not only is parchment paper great for ensuring that delicate cookies don't stick or break when you try to remove them, it makes cleanup that much quicker. Just crumple the sheet up, throw it in the garbage, and put your baking pan away. Parchment paper is available in rolls in the supermarket and in sheets at baking supply stores.

Pastry brush: Necessary for applying egg wash to puff pastry.

Pie pan: A 9-inch pie pan with angled sides (not straight sides like a cake pan) is a good thing to have around if you get the urge for Peanut Butter Pie. I use a glass pan, which produces the crispest crust.

Ramekins: Individual-size ceramic ramekins come in handy for custards and soufflés. I like the way these simple desserts look when transported to the table intact rather than messily ladled from a larger dish. Ramekins cost no more than a few dollars each and are available at any cookware shop. The most handy sizes are 6, 8, and 10 ounces.

Roasting pan: This makes a good water bath for custards and bread puddings. Use any pan you have around that will accommodate your ramekins or baking dish; just make sure that its sides are not much higher than your dessert dishes, since this might insulate your desserts too well from the heat of the oven and slow down cooking.

Rolling pin: Although you won't have time to roll out homemade pie dough or cookie dough if you are determined to prepare dessert in 15 minutes, you will need a rolling pin for store-bought all-butter puff pastry.

Saucepans: Saucepans in several sizes are necessary for making everything from Coconut Rice Pudding to Rum-Caramel Fondue. One of my favorites is a tiny butter warmer; this not only melts butter but heats small amounts of cream or jam, which tend to disappear across the bottom of a larger pan.

Spatulas: A rubber spatula is essential for scraping down the sides of a mixing bowl, folding ingredients together, and smoothing the surface of a cake batter before it goes into the oven. A metal spatula is essential for removing cookies from a cookie sheet. Used less frequently, a metal offset or icing spatula is convenient for smoothing icings and spreading fillings.

Springform pans: These cake pans with removable sides take the anxiety out of unmolding a cheesecake or a chocolate mousse cake. I have them in several sizes, from

6 inches, which will serve four nicely, to 10 inches, which might serve a dozen.

Strainer: A fine-mesh strainer performs a number of important tasks—straining custards, sifting confectioners' sugar, draining fruit so it doesn't make a tart crust soggy.

Tart pans: These fluted pans with removable bottoms have multiple uses. Whatever your preferred dessert flavors—fruit, chocolate, nuts, cream—a tart shell can accommodate them. Shortbread cookies baked in a tart pan have lovely fluted edges and are easy to cut and remove. For entertaining, I sometimes bake individual tarts rather than one large one; dessert seems somehow more exciting when everyone gets his or her own. I have a 9-inch, 8-inch, and half a dozen 4-inch pans that I use constantly.

Vegetable peeler: Although you can use a paring knife to peel fruit, a vegetable peeler is quicker and safer. I swear by the Oxo Good Grips peeler, the one with the soft black rubber handle, as the easiest and fastest to use.

Waffle iron: Not an essential, but nice to have if you want to make the two waffle dessert recipes in the book.

Wire racks: Even if you are absolutely desperate for a cookie or a piece of cake, it's usually a good idea for safety's sake to let your baked goods cool on a rack for a few minutes before eating.

Wire whisk: I have whisks in several sizes to banish lumps from tiny amounts of melting gelatin, reasonable amounts of melting bittersweet chocolate, and industrial-size batches of butterscotch pudding.

INGREDIENTS FOR INSTANT GRATIFICATION

Tortuous preparations of multiple components may disguise an elaborate cake's inferior ingredients. Who's going to know that you used "white confection" instead of real white chocolate with cocoa butter in a creation that also contains sponge layers, raspberry preserves, and kirsch syrup? No such sleight of hand is possible with simple desserts.

The recipes in this book call for a minimum of ingredients, and each one is going to be on display. So there's nowhere to hide if your strawberries aren't ripe or your walnuts have been sitting on the shelf too long. Making great, quick desserts doesn't require kitchen skill as much as it requires shopping know-how. Which brand of cocoa powder is the richest? Is this the right time of year for great blueberries, or should you stick with Granny Smith apples? Always buy the best, and you are well on your way to producing amazing desserts.

This does not mean that you'll have to waste any time looking for obscure specialty items. *Instant Gratification* is about simple cooking. None of the recipes require hard-to-find ingredients; you'll be able to buy everything you need at the supermarket or local gourmet shop. Just be sure that you are discriminating. If you want to treat your guests to Parmesan Shortbreads with Red Wine Strawberries, use imported Reggiano cheese rather than a characterless domestic variety. It will make a difference. Raspberry-Cheese Turnovers will be better if made with fresh raspberries and all-butter puff pastry rather than frozen fruit and vegetable-shortening dough. In other words, when your ingredients have integrity, your dessert is guaranteed to be delicious, even if it took you only 15 minutes to prepare. It is as simple as that.

Bread: My freezer is stocked with a variety of artisanal breads that can be defrosted for quick desserts, and I never throw out any leftovers. Rustic white bread makes incomparable crumbs for Plum Brown Betty. Slices of brioche can be transformed into Dessert French Toast with Almond Cream. Croissants make superb bread pudding.

Butter: I always use unsalted butter, especially in desserts. It has a purer flavor than the salted variety, and if salt is necessary in a dessert, you can always add it yourself.

Chocolate: For many people, chocolate *is* dessert. I prefer bittersweet to semisweet for its deep chocolate flavor, but semisweet is fine if you prefer. Ghirardelli makes good-quality bittersweet and semisweet varieties and is widely available in supermarkets. Make sure that any white chocolate you buy has cocoa butter high on its ingredients list. Otherwise, it will have a chalky rather than smooth consistency and taste more like sugar than cocoa butter. I buy Lindt white chocolate at my supermarket.

Cornmeal: Yellow cornmeal adds great color and crunch to a variety of cakes and cookies. I find white cornmeal too bland for baking. When available, I buy stone-ground cornmeal, but Quaker and other national brands stocked in the cereal aisle are just fine. Instant polenta, cornmeal that has been precooked and needs only to be rehydrated, is great for quick desserts like Indian Pudding.

Crème fraîche: Crème fraîche is heavy cream that has been slightly soured by adding a bit of buttermilk or sour cream and is allowed to stand overnight to thicken. It is also available, already whipped and ready to serve as a dessert garnish, in the dairy case of cheese shops, gourmet stores, and many supermarkets.

Dried fruit: In the dead of winter, high-quality dried fruit is a wonderful alternative to lackluster fresh fruit. Dried fruit is sometimes quicker to prepare than its fresh counterpart. Dried cherries have already been pitted and are ready to use; apricots, peaches, and prunes have been peeled and pitted and just need to be chopped before being added to cakes and cookies. Buy dried fruit that is still moist, not leathery and hard. Keep it well wrapped in plastic and stored in airtight containers to preserve flavor and freshness.

Eggs: All recipes in this book have been tested with large eggs. There is no difference in flavor or quality between brown and white eggs; use whichever color you like.

Espresso powder: A terrific way to add depth to many chocolate desserts. Look for espresso powder in the coffee aisle of the supermarket.

Extracts: You probably have pure vanilla extract in your pantry (avoid artificial vanilla). If you are interested in quickly expanding your flavoring options, invest in small bottles of pure almond, mint, and maple as well.

Flour: I use either King Arthur or Hecker's unbleached all-purpose flour. When I want a dessert to have a finer texture, I use Soft-as-Silk cake flour (not self-rising), which has a lower protein content and produces very light baked goods.

Fruit: I am lucky enough to live in a farming community where, for several months of the year, locally grown fruit is abundant and available. Whenever possible, I take advantage of just-picked apples, peaches, and berries. They always taste better than fruit that's been trucked or flown in from somewhere far away. That said, it is delightfully convenient to have a well-stocked supermarket with an incredible variety of both familiar and exotic items to choose from. I am especially fond of tropical fruit that I never sampled as a kid—mango, starfruit, papaya, and those incredible golden pineapples from Costa Rica. Wherever you buy your fresh fruit, use common sense and your sense of smell to determine flavor and ripeness. Strawberries in the middle of the winter are probably not a good bet. Ditto plums that are rock hard and smell like the plastic trays they've been packed in.

Gelatin: Flavorless gelatin magically turns liquids into semisolid desserts. It comes packaged in individual packets of powder, and must be dissolved in liquid and then gently heated before being added to puddings and mousses. Gelatin desserts are easier to put together and harder to ruin than egg-based custards, which have a tendency to curdle if not watched carefully.

Graham cracker crumbs: Graham cracker crumbs are indispensable for making quick pie and tart crusts. I buy them preground in the baking aisle of the supermarket, but if I run out, I just raid my daughter's supply of graham cracker cookies and grind them in the food processor.

Ice cream: High-quality store-bought ice cream is a great boon in putting together homemade desserts. I always buy luxury brands with high butterfat content. The richer the ice cream, the better the dessert.

Liqueurs, wines, and spirits: I keep small bottles of Kahlúa, Grand Marnier, dark rum, and brandy around to add depth and flavor quickly and easily to all kinds of desserts, from Mango-Rum Fool to Chocolate "Crepes" with Kahlúa Cream. Leftover cupfuls of wine and champagne can also be put to good use, so keep them around in case you get the urge for Blackberries with Champagne Sabayon.

Mascarpone: Like crème fraîche, this Italian cream cheese is becoming widely available at cheese shops and supermarkets throughout the country. Mascarpone has a milder flavor than American cream cheese and an incredibly creamy texture. It is an interesting substitute for whipped cream in many desserts.

Nabisco Famous Chocolate Wafers: When I'm not using graham crackers for a pie crust, chances are I'm using these cookies. Ground in a food processor and mixed with melted butter, they make a surprisingly rich and chocolatey container for a variety of ingredients from sweetened pecans to mascarpone and raspberries.

Nuts: Without a large variety of shelled nuts, I wouldn't be able to make many of my favorite quick desserts. There is no quicker pie filling than pecan halves straight from the bag and no more convenient way to add flavor and texture to cookies than with a handful of chopped cashews. Nuts are expensive and go rancid quickly. Still, I like to have a lot on hand, so I buy large bags at my local warehouse discount store and keep them in the freezer to preserve freshness.

Peanut butter: Most supermarket peanut butters are too sweet for my taste. I use Smucker's Natural peanut butter, which doesn't contain corn syrup or any other additives. I don't recommend peanut butter ground fresh at supermarkets or natural foods stores, since it always seems too coarse and grainy for most desserts.

Puff pastry: Prepared frozen puff pastry is a real boon to the time-pressed baker. As good as—if not better than—anything you could make yourself, it provides the essential crispy-buttery component to innumerable quick desserts. Buy a brand such as Dufour, made with butter rather than vegetable shortening, for best results.

Sugars: I use granulated sugar for basic baking, light and dark brown sugars when I want a hint of molasses in my desserts, and confectioners' sugar for sweetening whipped cream and decorating finished cakes, soufflés, crepes, etc. Sugar keeps indefinitely in airtight containers, so, for the sake of convenience, I always keep a good supply in my pantry.

Unsweetened cocoa powder: All of the recipes in this book have been tested with Dutch-process Pernigotti cocoa, a brand unsurpassed in richness. Droste, another widely available brand, is also very good.

Vanilla beans: For most desserts, a teaspoon or so of pure vanilla extract will do the trick. Every once in a while, however, I like to use the seeds from whole vanilla beans for their intense flavor and the attractive flecks they leave in a dessert. Vanilla beans are simple to use. Carefully split the bean in half lengthwise using a sharp paring knife and scrape the seeds from the inside of the bean with the blade of the knife. In my opinion, this single ingredient transforms unremarkable sweets like bread pudding and plain cupcakes into special desserts.

WHEN YOU'VE GOT TO HAVE IT

UNBELIEVABLE DESSERTS IN 15 MINUTES FLAT

SPICED MEXICAN CHOCOLATE PUDDING

CHOCOLATE-CHERRY BRIOCHE SANDWICHES

AMAZING ALMOST INSTANT WARM BROWNIES AND ICE CREAM

SAUTÉED BROWN SUGAR BANANAS OVER COCONUT ICE CREAM

TINY COCONUT MACAROONS

MINI PEANUT BUTTER CUPS

BROWN SUGAR MINI CUPCAKES

BITTERSWEET CHOCOLATE WAFFLES WITH MINT CHOCOLATE CHIP ICE CREAM

PECAN WAFFLES WITH RUM RAISIN ICE CREAM

DESSERT FRENCH TOAST WITH ALMOND CREAM

APRICOTS STUFFED WITH ALMOND PASTE

WARM PEACH GRATIN

WONTON PLUM "SHORTCAKES"

WONTON "CANAPÉS" WITH CRÈME FRAÎCHE AND DICED MANGO

SOMETIMES THE DESIRE FOR DESSERT MUST BE SATISFIED quickly. Anyone who has ever mixed a batch of Tollhouse batter primarily in order to enjoy the raw dough knows what I mean. The desserts in this chapter offer the same instant gratification as cookie dough, without the sick feeling that usually accompanies such an indulgence. In the time it takes to gather and mix the ingredients for chocolate chip cookies, you could be eating any of these wonderful (and fully cooked) creations.

What kinds of desserts can be ready to eat in 15 minutes? In general, they contain just a few ingredients, don't require a lot of preparation or cooking, and are best consumed warm. Ideally, 15-minute desserts deliver pure, uncomplicated pleasure and satisfy the elemental need to get it while it's hot.

I begin the chapter with a definitive recipe for instant gratification, Spiced Mexican Chocolate Pudding. Made from a few items I usually stock in my pantry and refrigerator, it satisfies that after-dinner, "I need something sweet" feeling like nothing else. Especially on chilly nights when the craving for something warm matches the craving for something sweet, this quick dessert is just about perfect.

While I never use cake mixes or canned frosting, I do think that there are a few prepared ingredients that make "instant" desserts possible. Now that wonderful artisanal loaves are widely available at local bakeries and many supermarkets, I always seem to have an extra chunk of bread around. Recalling that each loaf can cost upward of five dollars, the cheapskate in me feels the need to use every bit of it. Thus, the recipe for Chocolate-Cherry Brioche Sandwiches. These make great afternoon or coffee-break snacks, and are also fitting at the end of a light family meal that doesn't include a lot of heavy starches. Kids are often amazed and delighted by the transformation of bread into dessert. Thrifty parents won't complain either when their costly leftovers are put to such use.

Super-premium ice cream is another essential ingredient for instant gratification. Of course, with so many fantastic flavors available, any accompaniment that you bother to make had better be as good as Ben and Jerry's Cherry

Garcia or you might as well just eat your ice cream unadorned and straight from the container. I include two recipes that definitely are worth the extra minutes. Sautéed Brown Sugar Bananas are so delectable I almost forget that they are intended as an ice cream topping and find myself eating them hot from the sauté pan. Microwave brownies, made especially to accompany ice cream, are shockingly quick and just perfect when you really feel like indulging. In practically the time it takes to let the Häagen-Dazs soften up for scooping, you can mix, bake, and portion these out in your favorite sundae bowls.

When I want something freshly baked but fast, I go for bite-size cupcakes and tiny cookies, which cook in about 10 minutes and can be eaten straight from the pan. Tiny Coconut Macaroons deliver pure, sweet flavor—probably because they contain only 4 ingredients. Simple cupcakes sweetened with brown sugar or combining peanut butter and chocolate somehow taste better when baked in miniature muffin tins. Alternatively, breakfast specialties like waffles or French toast, garnished with whipped cream or ice cream, offer the same satisfaction as baked goods without the baking and cooling time. Of course, if you are a real voluptuary, you may skip the bran cereal and serve the waffle and French toast recipes here for breakfast.

The last couple of recipes in the chapter are just as quick and simple as the recipes that precede them, but are unusual or impressive enough that you might want to save them for entertaining. Apricots Stuffed with Almond Paste are exotic-tasting morsels that will make your guests feel pampered and special. Warm Peach Gratin is a perfect summer dessert for a casual dinner party. Store-bought wonton wrappers provide a crisp pastry counterpart—without any rolling or baking—for different fruit-and-cream combinations in the final two recipes.

Whether you are fighting the cookie dough craving or planning a real, grown-up dinner party, there is no reason that you can't gratify any dessert need almost instantly with one of the recipes below.

Other desserts that are ready to eat in 15 minutes:

Spiced Mexican Chocolate Pudding

In my opinion, this is the perfect quick dessert. Rich, warm pudding satisfies the fundamental need for chocolate; cinnamon gives it a twist. The beautiful part is that you don't even have to wait for the pudding to cool off—stirring in the chocolate at the end lowers the temperature so that it is perfect for eating just as soon as the chocolate is melted.

MAKES 4 SERVINGS

EQUIPMENT

Measuring cups and measuring spoons
Chef's knife
Cutting board
Medium-size saucepan
Wire whisk
Rubber spatula
4 dessert goblets

INGREDIENTS

¼ cup cornstarch
6 tablespoons sugar
½ teaspoon ground cinnamon
1¼ cups heavy cream
1¼ cups milk
6 ounces bittersweet chocolate, finely chopped
1 tablespoon butter

1. Combine the cornstarch, sugar, and cinnamon in the saucepan. Whisk in ½ cup of the heavy cream until the mixture is smooth.

   Add the remaining ¾ cup heavy cream and the milk and bring to a boil, whisking constantly. Continue to cook over medium-high heat, whisking, until the mixture thickens, 3 to 4 minutes.

2. Remove from the heat and whisk in the chocolate and butter, continuing to whisk until all the chocolate and butter have melted and the pudding is very smooth.

3. Scrape into the dessert goblets with the rubber spatula and serve warm, or refrigerate up to 24 hours and serve cold.

Chocolate-Cherry Brioche Sandwiches

Once when I had some leftover brioche, I put together a few of these simple, sweet sandwiches as an afternoon snack for myself and my daughter. Rich egg bread is best, but children (and grown-up kids) will love any soft fresh white bread stuck together with a layer of chocolate.

MAKES 2 SERVINGS

EQUIPMENT

Measuring spoons

Butter warmer or small saucepan

Wooden spoon

Knife

INGREDIENTS

2 ounces bittersweet chocolate

2 tablespoons cherry preserves

Four ½-inch-thick slices brioche or challah

1. Combine the chocolate and preserves in the butter warmer or over low heat. Heat, stirring frequently, until the chocolate is completely melted.

2. Spread some of the chocolate-cherry mixture on two of the slices of brioche. Top with the remaining slices. Serve immediately.

Amazing Almost Instant
Warm Brownies and Ice Cream

In general, I disapprove of microwave baking because the microwave can't produce a crisp exterior or beautiful brown crust. This recipe is the exception. The warm, soft brownies provide the perfect base for slowly melting ice cream. A warning—these brownies *must* be eaten warm (for most chocolate lovers this shouldn't be a problem); like a lot of food cooked in the microwave, they will become rock-hard if allowed to cool.

MAKES 6 SERVINGS

EQUIPMENT

Measuring spoons and measuring cups
8-inch square glass baking dish
Nonstick cooking spray
Butter warmer or small saucepan
Whisk
Large bowl
Rubber spatula
Toothpick
Wire rack
Knife
6 dessert bowls

INGREDIENTS

¼ cup (½ stick) butter
2 large eggs
1 teaspoon pure vanilla extract
1 cup sugar
½ cup unsweetened cocoa powder
½ cup all-purpose flour
1 pint ice cream, softened a bit (I like coffee, cherry vanilla, or mint chocolate chip for this)

1. Spray the baking dish with cooking spray. Melt the butter in the butter warmer or saucepan.

2. Whisk together the melted butter, eggs, and vanilla in the bowl. Stir in the sugar, cocoa, and flour until well combined.

3. Scrape the batter with the spatula into the prepared dish. Microwave on high power until the toothpick inserted into the center comes out clean, 4 to 7 minutes depending on the power and size of your oven. Let cool on the wire rack for 5 minutes.

4. Cut the brownies into 12 squares. Place 2 squares into each of the dessert bowls. Top with a scoop of ice cream and serve immediately.

Sautéed Brown Sugar Bananas over Coconut Ice Cream

One day when I was making some filling for banana tarts, I tasted the sautéed bananas. I halted my tart-making immediately and decided instead to use the bananas as an ice cream topping. Ben & Jerry's Coconut Cream Pie Ice Cream completed this quick dessert. Of course, any brand of vanilla or rum raisin is also outrageously good. Cool the bananas slightly so that they don't instantly turn your scoops of ice cream into puddles. They should feel just warm (not hot) to the touch to make a perfect sundae.

MAKES 4 SERVINGS

EQUIPMENT
Measuring spoons
Medium-size skillet
Paring knife
Spoon
Rubber spatula
Small shallow bowl
4 dessert bowls

INGREDIENTS
2 tablespoons butter
2 medium-size ripe bananas
2 tablespoons firmly packed light brown sugar
1 pint coconut cream pie, vanilla, or rum raisin ice cream, softened a bit

1. Heat the butter in the skillet over medium heat. While the butter is melting, peel and slice the bananas into ¼-inch-thick rounds.

2. Add the bananas and brown sugar to the skillet and cook, stirring frequently with a spoon, until the bananas are softened (but not so mushy that they are falling apart) and the sugar is dissolved, 2 to 4 minutes. Remove from the heat, scrape into a shallow bowl, and let stand until just warm to the touch, 2 to 3 minutes.

3. Divide the ice cream among the dessert bowls. Spoon some bananas and sauce over each and serve immediately.

Tiny Coconut Macaroons

Unsweetened coconut (available at natural foods stores and many supermarkets) makes the best macaroons, with a lot of pure coconut flavor. Mix the batter in 3 minutes and bake for another 10 to 12 for the quickest cookies ever.

MAKES ABOUT 20 COOKIES

EQUIPMENT

Measuring spoons and measuring cups
Baking sheet
Parchment paper
Medium-size bowl
Rubber spatula
Teaspoon
Wire rack

INGREDIENTS

6 tablespoons sugar
1¼ cups unsweetened shredded coconut
1 large egg white
½ teaspoon pure vanilla extract

1. Preheat the oven to 375 degrees. Line the baking sheet with parchment paper.

2. Combine the sugar, coconut, egg white, and vanilla in the bowl and mix with the spatula.

3. Drop heaping teaspoonfuls of the batter onto the prepared baking sheet. Bake until golden, 10 to 12 minutes. Slide the parchment onto the wire rack and let cool for a minute or two before eating.

Mini Peanut Butter Cups

It is possible to have finished cupcakes in 15 minutes, if you make them from the simplest batter and bake them in mini muffin tins Here, a peanut-butter-and-chocolate-chip batter is whipped up in the food processor in under 5 minutes and baked for just about 10 minutes.

MAKES 24 MINI CUPCAKES

EQUIPMENT

Measuring cups and measuring spoons

Butter knife

Two 12-cup mini muffin tins

Nonstick cooking spray

Food processor fitted with metal blade

Rubber spatula

Cake tester

Wire rack

INGREDIENTS

½ cup plus 2 tablespoons all-purpose flour

¼ cup plus 2 tablespoons firmly packed light brown sugar

¾ teaspoon baking powder

½ teaspoon salt

¼ cup plus 2 tablespoons milk

3 tablespoons peanut butter

1 large egg yolk

2 tablespoons unsalted butter, softened

1 teaspoon pure vanilla extract

½ cup miniature chocolate chips

1. Preheat the oven to 350 degrees. Spray the muffin tins with nonstick cooking spray.

2. Combine the flour, sugar, baking powder, and salt in the work bowl of the food processor and pulse once or twice. Add the milk, peanut butter, egg yolk, butter, and vanilla and process until smooth, scraping down the side of the bowl with the spatula once or twice. Add the chocolate chips and pulse once or twice to mix.

3. Fill the muffin cups about three-quarters full and bake until risen and the cake tester inserted into the center of one of the cupcakes comes out clean, 10 to 12 minutes. Remove from the pan and cool for a minute or two on the wire rack before eating.

Brown Sugar Mini Cupcakes

Sometimes only something sweet and hot from the oven will do, even if you've just got to have it in 15 minutes. These dark, chewy mouthfuls are the essence of home baking. This ultra-comforting recipe is adapted from one in *The Fannie Farmer Cookbook*. Take the editors' advice and spread a little butter on the cupcakes before popping them into your mouth.

MAKES 24 MINI CUPCAKES

EQUIPMENT

Measuring cups and measuring spoons
Butter knife
Two 12-cup mini muffin tins
Nonstick cooking spray
Food processor fitted with metal blade
Rubber spatula
Wire rack

INGREDIENTS

½ cup plus 2 tablespoons all-purpose flour
½ cup firmly packed dark brown sugar
¾ teaspoon baking powder
⅛ teaspoon salt
1 large egg yolk
¼ cup plus 2 tablespoons milk
3 tablespoons unsalted butter, softened
1 teaspoon pure vanilla extract

1. Preheat the oven to 350 degrees. Spray the muffin tins with nonstick cooking spray.

2. Combine the flour, sugar, baking powder, and salt in the work bowl of the food processor and pulse once or twice. Add the egg yolk, milk, butter, and vanilla and process until smooth, scraping down the side of the bowl with the spatula, once or twice as necessary.

3. Fill the muffin cups about three-quarters full and bake until risen and a toothpick inserted into the center of one of the cupcakes comes out clean, 10 to 12 minutes. Remove from the pan and let cool for a minute or two on the wire rack before eating.

Store-bought ice cream is not the only item that can quickly be turned into a satisfying dessert. Brewed coffee, something that almost everyone can make, is a great base for a number of sweet drinks that can take the place of dessert. (If you're going to drink a cup of strong coffee with a shot of Kahlúa and a dollop of sweetened whipped cream, dessert seems superfluous.) I always use strong French roast coffee or espresso; they stand up best when paired with other strong flavors. If I'm going to drink one of these after dinner, I use decaf to prevent sleeplessness.

◆

Coffee with Chocolate Cream: Melt 1 ounce bittersweet or semisweet chocolate in ½ cup hot half-and-half or milk. Stir in ¼ cup hot coffee or espresso.

Irish Coffee: Stir 1 to 2 tablespoons Irish whiskey into ¾ cup hot coffee. Top with sweetened whipped cream.

Amaretto Coffee: Stir 1 to 2 tablespoons Amaretto or other almond-flavored liqueur into ¾ cup hot coffee. Top with sweetened whipped cream and a little grated orange zest.

Orange Coffee with Cardamom Cream: Stir 1 tablespoon Grand Marnier or other orange-flavored liqueur into ¾ cup hot coffee. Top with a dollop of sweetened whipped cream. Sprinkle with ground cardamom.

Cinnamon-Spiced Coffee with Dark Rum: Stir 1 to 2 tablespoons dark rum into ¾ cup hot coffee. Top with a dollop of sweetened whipped cream and a cinnamon stick for stirring and flavoring.

Espresso Milk Shake: Combine ¾ cup milk, 1 shot (about ¼ cup) cooled brewed espresso, and 2 scoops softened coffee ice cream in a blender and blend until smooth.

Iced Mocha: Stir ½ ounce bittersweet or semisweet chocolate into ¾ cup hot coffee until melted. Let cool slightly. Combine the coffee, ¼ cup cold heavy cream, and 4 ice cubes in a blender and blend until smooth.

Bittersweet Chocolate Waffles with Mint Chocolate Chip Ice Cream

Warm chocolate waffles make a great base for ice cream. I have a Belgian waffle iron that makes 2 large waffles at a time. This recipe makes 6 waffles in my machine, but might make more or less in yours, depending on its size.

MAKES 6 SERVINGS

EQUIPMENT

Measuring cups and measuring spoons

Waffle iron

Nonstick cooking spray

Double boiler or medium-size saucepan and
    medium-size stainless steel bowl

Chef's knife

Cutting board

Wire whisk

Medium-size bowl

Spoon

Fork

6 dessert plates

INGREDIENTS

4 ounces bittersweet chocolate

1/2 cup (1 stick) unsalted butter

1/2 cup sugar

4 large eggs

2 teaspoons pure vanilla extract

1/4 cup milk

1 cup all-purpose flour

1 teaspoon baking powder

1/2 teaspoon salt

1 pint mint chocolate chip ice cream, softened
    a bit

1. Heat the waffle iron and spray the grids with nonstick cooking spray.

2. Put 1 inch of water into the bottom of the double boiler or saucepan and bring to a bare simmer. Finely chop the chocolate. Combine the chocolate and butter in the top of the double boiler or in the stainless steel bowl and place it on top of the simmering water, making sure that the water doesn't touch the bowl. Heat, whisking occasionally,

until the chocolate and butter are completely melted.

3. Whisk together the sugar, eggs, vanilla, and milk in the medium-size bowl. Whisk in the chocolate mixture. Stir in the flour, baking powder, and salt.

4. Pour some batter over the grids. Close the waffles iron and cook until well done. Remove the waffles with a fork. Repeat as necessary until your batter is used up.

5. Divide the waffles among the dessert plates. Top with a scoop or two of ice cream. Serve immediately.

Pecan Waffles with Rum Raisin Ice Cream

Brown sugar and pecans give these dessert waffles appealing crunch and sweetness. They are not too sweet, however, to serve as a base for your favorite super-premium ice cream.

MAKES 6 SERVINGS

EQUIPMENT

Measuring cups and measuring spoons

Waffle iron

Nonstick cooking spray

Butter warmer or small saucepan

Food processor fitted with metal blade

Small bowl

Fork

6 dessert plates

INGREDIENTS

½ cup (1 stick) unsalted butter

½ cup pecans

½ cup plus 2 tablespoons firmly packed dark brown
   sugar

2 large eggs

1 cup milk

1 cup all-purpose flour

2 teaspoons baking powder

½ teaspoon salt

¾ teaspoon ground cinnamon

1 pint rum-raisin or vanilla ice cream, softened a bit

1. Heat the waffle iron and spray the grids with nonstick cooking spray.

2. Melt the butter in the butter warmer or saucepan.

3. Place the pecans in the work bowl of the food processor and process until finely chopped (do not grind too fine). Transfer to the bowl and set aside.

4. Add the brown sugar, eggs, milk, and melted butter to the food processor (there is no need

to wash it) and process to combine. Add the nuts, flour, baking powder, salt, and cinnamon and pulse two or three times to combine.

5. Pour some batter over the grids. Close the waffle iron and cook until well done. Remove the waffles with a fork. Repeat as necessary until your batter is used up.

6. Divide the waffles among the dessert plates. Top with a scoop or two of ice cream. Serve immediately.

5 MINUTES EXTRA

Warm fruit toppings are great on dessert waffles. With the pecan variety, I like to sauté 4 peeled, cored, and thinly sliced apples in ¼ cup (½ stick) unsalted butter and ¼ cup plus 2 tablespoons granulated sugar. When the apples are slightly softened, but not mushy or falling apart, 5 to 7 minutes, I add ¼ cup heavy cream and ¼ cup dark rum and stir until slightly thickened. The topping can be used on its own or with the ice cream.

Dessert French Toast with Almond Cream

Another breakfast classic, served up as dessert (actually, in France, French toast is frequently served as dessert). Here, bread is caramelized with a coating of confectioners' sugar and garnished with almond-flavored whipped cream. Rich egg bread like brioche or challah is essential here. Watch the toast carefully—the confectioners' sugar will make it brown quickly and you don't want it to burn.

MAKES 4 SERVINGS

EQUIPMENT

Measuring cups and measuring spoons
Butter knife
2 medium-size bowls
Electric mixer fitted with whisk attachment
Slotted spatula
Large plate
Large skillet
4 dessert plates

INGREDIENTS

¾ cup heavy cream
¼ cup plus 1 tablespoon confectioners' sugar
½ teaspoon pure almond extract
2 large eggs
2 teaspoons pure vanilla extract
1 cup milk

½ cup granulated sugar
Four 1-inch-thick slices brioche or challah
2 tablespoons unsalted butter

1. Combine the heavy cream, 1 tablespoon of the confectioners' sugar, and the almond extract in one of the bowls and beat with the mixture until it holds stiff peaks. Refrigerate until ready to use.

2. Combine the eggs, vanilla, milk, and granulated sugar in the other bowl and whisk to combine. Dip each piece of bread in the mixture and remove with the slotted spatula to the plate. Sprinkle each piece with ½ tablespoon of the confectioners' sugar.

3. Melt the butter in the skillet over medium heat. Place the bread, sugared side down, in the skillet and cook until deep golden, 3 to 4 minutes. Sprinkle each slice with another ½ tablespoon confectioners' sugar, turn, and cook until golden, about 3 minutes.

4. Transfer each slice of French toast to a dessert plate, top with a dollop of almond cream, and serve immediately.

Toast ¼ cup sliced almonds on a baking sheet in a preheated 350-degree oven until golden, about 5 minutes. Garnish the French toast and cream with the toasted almonds.

Apricots Stuffed with Almond Paste

This recipe, borrowed from my first book, *Cool Kitchen,* is simple but unusual. You'll need large, moist dried apricots here. I buy the ones imported from Australia. Serve with a glass of sweet wine or one or two other little bites— Anise-Flavored Butter Cookies (page 174) and Sweet and Spicy Pecan Brittle (page 186) would make a good assortment.

MAKES 12 STUFFED APRICOTS

EQUIPMENT

Measuring cups and measuring spoons
Sharp paring knife
Food processor fitted with metal blade
Rubber spatula
Small bowl
Spoon

INGREDIENTS

12 large dried apricots
⅓ cup blanched almonds
2 tablespoons confectioners' sugar
2 teaspoons water

1. Slice apricots almost in half with a sharp paring knife.

2. Place the almonds and sugar in the work bowl of the food processor. Process until the nuts are very finely ground. Add the water and process until a smooth paste forms. Scrape the almond paste with the spatula into the small bowl.

3. Spoon some almond paste onto the center of each split apricot, pressing together the halves so that a little bit of the paste squeezes out around the edges (you'll get an Oreo sandwich effect). The stuffed apricots can be stored in an airtight container at room temperature for 1 day.

Warm Peach Gratin

Sour cream whisked together with a little bit of sugar makes a simple "sauce" for a quick fruit gratin. This dessert depends on very sweet, ripe fruit to contrast with the tangy sour cream, so shop accordingly. Make sure the fruit is at room temperature, so your gratin will be warm, not chilled, when you serve it.

MAKES 6 SERVINGS

EQUIPMENT

Measuring cups and measuring spoons

Wire whisk

Small bowl

Cutting board

Paring knife

9-inch round glass or ceramic baking dish or pie plate

Spoon

INGREDIENTS

1 cup sour cream

¼ cup heavy cream

¼ cup granulated sugar

1½ pounds ripe peaches (3 or 4 medium-size), at room temperature

2 tablespoons firmly packed light brown sugar

1. Position the oven rack as close to the heating element as possible and preheat the broiler.

2. Whisk together the sour cream, heavy cream, and granulated sugar in the bowl.

3. Halve, pit, and slice each peach into eighths. Arrange the peach slices on the bottom of the baking dish or pie plate. Spoon the sour cream mixture over the fruit and smooth with the back of the spoon. Sprinkle the brown sugar evenly across the top of the sour cream.

4. Broil until the brown sugar is melted, 2 to 3 minutes. Serve immediately.

5 MINUTES EXTRA

For a more refined dessert, peel the peaches before pitting and slicing.

Wonton Plum "Shortcakes"

Wonton wrappers, available in the produce section of most supermarkets, are a truly amazing resource if you want to put an impressive dessert on the table in less than 15 minutes. Here, I sandwich some ginger-macerated plums and whipped cream between two crisp, sugared wontons to create a "shortcake"-type dessert without any real baking. You can toast the wontons in advance and keep them in an airtight container for several hours until serving. Likewise, you can macerate the fruit several hours early, and keep refrigerated until serving. Freeze extra wrappers (they come in packages of 50 or so) for dessert emergencies.

MAKES 4 SERVINGS

EQUIPMENT

Measuring spoons and measuring cups

Butter warmer or small saucepan

Cutting board

Paring knife

2 medium-size bowls

Pastry brush

Baking sheet

Electric mixer fitted with whisk attachment

4 dessert plates

Spoon

INGREDIENTS

2 tablespoons unsalted butter

2 medium-size plums

1/4 cup sugar

1/2 teaspoon ground ginger

8 wonton wrappers

1 cup heavy cream

1/4 teaspoon pure vanilla extract

1. Preheat the oven to 425 degrees. Melt the butter in the butter warmer or saucepan.

2. Halve and pit each plum, and slice each half into 6 wedges. Place the wedges, 2 tablespoons of the sugar, and the ginger in one of the bowls and toss to combine.

3. Brush both sides of each wonton wrapper with a little melted butter. Place on the baking

sheet and sprinkle them with 1 tablespoon of the sugar. Bake until golden brown, 3 to 4 minutes. Watch them carefully; after they brown, they will burn quickly.

4. Combine the heavy cream, vanilla, and the remaining 1 tablespoon sugar in the other bowl and whip with the mixer until soft peaks form.

5. To assemble the dessert, place 1 wonton on each of the dessert plates. Place 3 plum slices on top of each wonton, and top with a dollop of the whipped cream. Lay the remaining 4 wontons on top of each pile of fruit and cream, and place 3 plum slices and a dollop of whipped cream on the second wonton. Serve immediately.

Wonton "Canapés" with Crème Fraîche and Diced Mango

Almost every day I am amazed by some new, high-quality ingredient available at my local supermarket. When my husband reported that he had spotted some crème fraîche in the dairy case, I immediately ran out to buy some. In the produce aisle, I grabbed a mango and some wontons, and this dessert is the result. If crème fraîche hasn't made it to your supermarket, substitute sour cream.

MAKES 4 SERVINGS

EQUIPMENT

Measuring spoons and measuring cups
Large skillet
Spatula
Large plate
Chef's knife
Cutting board
4 dessert plates
Spoon

INGREDIENTS

3 tablespoons unsalted butter
8 wonton wrappers
1/3 cup sugar
1 small ripe mango
5 tablespoons crème fraîche or sour cream
Pinch of 5-spice powder (optional)

1. Melt the butter in the skillet over medium heat. Add the wontons and fry, turning occasionally, until they just begin to color. Sprinkle the sugar over the wontons and cook, turning frequently, until the wontons are coated with the sugar and golden brown. Transfer to the plate and let cool.

2. Peel the mango and remove the flesh from the pit (see page 124). Cut the flesh into 1/2-inch dice.

3. Spread a scant 2 teaspoons of the crème fraîche on each cooled wonton. Top with some diced mango. Sprinkle with 5-spice powder if desired. Serve immediately on the dessert plates.

EASY

AS

PIE

APPLE "PIZZA" FOR TWO

PEACH AND SPICE "PIZZA" FOR TWO

QUICKEST PECAN TART

MAPLE-PECAN TART

SOURDOUGH NECTARINE TARTS

PECAN-CARAMEL-FUDGE PIE

PEANUT BUTTER PIE

COCOA MASCARPONE AND RASPBERRY TART WITH A
CHOCOLATE-ALMOND CRUST

WHITE CHOCOLATE–MINT TART WITH STRAWBERRIES

BLUEBERRY-COCONUT TART

OAT-CRISPED PEARS WITH SOUR CREAM

STRAWBERRY COBBLER WITH A LEMON BUTTER COOKIE CRUST

PEAR AND CORNMEAL COBBLER

BLUEBERRY-WALNUT CRISP

PEACH-CARDAMOM CRUMBLE

RASPBERRY BROWNIE COBBLER

PLUM BROWN BETTY

BITTERSWEET CHOCOLATE TURNOVERS

RASPBERRY-CHEESE TURNOVERS

APRICOT AND WHITE CHOCOLATE TURNOVERS

PUFF PASTRY APPLE TARTLETS

F OR SOME PEOPLE, NOTHING ANSWERS THE HUNGER FOR
dessert like a crisp pastry crust containing a fruity or creamy filling. Unfortunately for pie lovers, however, there is nothing quick or necessarily easy about making a conventional pie. Mixing and rolling the pastry alone takes well over 15 minutes. Precooking the filling ingredients, as is often required with fruit and custard pies, requires even more time.

The challenge of this chapter, then, was to come up with desserts that contained the elements of pie—crust and filling—without the work. None of the recipes that follow could be called a pie in the traditional sense. However, all approximate the pleasures of pie with their crispy-fruity or crispy-creamy contrasts. This is not to say that these desserts are pale imitations of the real thing. I do not use low-quality convenience foods and other cheap shortcuts to approximate time-consuming favorites. No "Mock Apple Pie" here! Desserts like White Chocolate–Mint Tart with Strawberries or Puff Pastry Apple Tartlets satisfy like pie and stand on their own merits as well.

There are a couple of absolutely delicious ways to dispense with traditional pie crust or minimize the work of filling a crust. For an Apple or Peach and Spice "Pizza" for Two, an easy pastry dough made with lots of butter and cream cheese is whipped up in the food processor and simply pressed it into a free-form circle. Mixing and hand shaping take just a few minutes. Because the peeling, pitting, and slicing of fruit can be prohibitively time-consuming, I keep these "pizzas" small. Peeling 1 apple for a romantic 2-person tart is a lot quicker than peeling a dozen for your Thanksgiving Day pie.

Crumb crusts have long been popular not only for their ease but for their crisp texture, which contrasts well with moist and gooey fillings and won't get soggy when refrigerated. If crumb crusts are combined with very simple fillings—unchopped nuts, uncooked fruit—the 15-minute goal can be reached. Because you can never have enough pecan pie, I've included a trio of recipes here that show off not just the versatility of the pecan (combined with brown sugar, maple syrup, or bittersweet chocolate) but the ease with which such a classic can be prepared. I keep fruit fillings simple, but hardly pedestrian. Blueberry-Coconut Tart is filled with a sublime mixture of berries, coconut, cream, and eggs. For Cocoa Mascarpone and Raspberry Tart with a Chocolate-Almond Crust, the filling is not baked; just spread the cocoa-flavored mascarpone across the bottom of the tart shell and scatter with berries.

A third option for pie lovers is the wide range of fruit cobblers, crisps, and brown betties that get their crispiness from a variety of toppings rather than from tricky and time-consuming pastry crusts. Peach-Cardamom Crumble is a minimalist version of pie. Thick wedges of fruit are topped with a sprinkling of flour, sugar, and butter that have been turned into crumbs in the food processor. A hint of cardamom gives this humble dessert an intriguing flavor and aroma. Plum Brown Betty utilizes ripe plums and the frugal cook's standby—bread crumbs—to accomplish a perfect balance of crispy and juicy. For Raspberry Brownie Cobbler, raspberries baked under a layer of brownie batter transform "cobbler" into a chocolate lover's dream. These homey desserts match the honest, comforting food that more and more time-pressed cooks

now choose to prepare, for both practical and nostalgic reasons, over fancy or complicated "gourmet" dishes.

Finally, store-bought puff pastry is a miracle ingredient for those of us who love a buttery, flaky crust but don't have the skill, time, or patience to make our own. All-butter brands such as Dufour, available at gourmet stores and many supermarkets, are just as good if not better than what you could make yourself. In fact, 4-star pastry chefs routinely buy puff pastry dough, saving time and ensuring uniform quality. Puff pastry requires some careful handling—it should be refrigerated or frozen before being baked, or it might melt instead of puff. Otherwise, it is simple to work with and incredibly delicious. Puff pastry freezes well, and I always keep some on hand for dessert emergencies. It's reassuring to know that with a little bit of planning you can be entirely self-sufficient with regard to bakery-quality desserts.

Other desserts that satisfy like pie:
Wonton Plum "Shortcakes" (page 36)
Cherry-Almond Frangipane Tarts (page 215)
Chocolate-Bourbon Tarts (page 217)

Apple "Pizza" for Two

A tart for two is quicker to prepare than a tart for 8. For one thing, you have to peel only 1 apple. There are other ways to save time without compromising quality: Slice the apple very thin so that it doesn't require sautéing first; make a rich cream cheese dough in the food processor in just a few seconds; instead of rolling it, simply pat it into a charmingly rustic circle. The parchment paper prevents any juices that might run off the apple slices from burning and blackening the crust.

MAKES 2 SERVINGS

EQUIPMENT

Measuring spoons and measuring cups

Baking sheet

Parchment paper

Vegetable peeler

Paring knife

Cutting board

Medium-size bowl

Spoon

Food processor fitted with metal blade

Strainer or colander

INGREDIENTS

1 large Granny Smith or other tart apple

2 tablespoons Calvados or brandy

2 tablespoons fresh lemon juice

½ cup plus 2 tablespoons sugar

⅛ teaspoon ground cinnamon

¼ cup cream cheese, chilled

¼ cup (½ stick) unsalted butter, chilled

½ cup all-purpose flour, plus more for shaping

Pinch of salt

1. Preheat the oven to 400 degrees. Line the baking sheet with parchment paper. Peel the apple and cut it in half. Remove the core with the knife. Slice each half into ¼-inch-thick slices. Put the slices in the bowl, add the Calvados or brandy, lemon juice, ¼ cup of the sugar, and the cinnamon. Stir to combine.

2. Place the cream cheese, butter, ½ cup flour, salt, and ¼ cup of the sugar in the work bowl of the food processor. Process until the dough

just comes together. It will be sticky. Sprinkle the parchment paper with flour. Turn the dough onto the parchment-lined baking sheet and, with floured hands, press it into a rough 8-inch circle.

3. Give the apples a stir and then turn them into the strainer or colander to drain the liquid. Arrange about three quarters of the slices in a

circle around the border of the dough, overlapping them slightly. Arrange the remaining slices in a smaller inner circle, again slightly overlapping them. Sprinkle the apples with the remaining 2 tablespoons sugar.

4. Bake until golden, 25 to 30 minutes. Serve warm or at room temperature.

Peach and Spice "Pizza" for Two

After the success of my apple pizza, I wanted to vary the recipe for a favorite summer fruit. Here, peaches are flavored with 5-spice powder (a blend of star anise, cloves, cinnamon, fennel, and pepper, conveniently packaged in 1 jar). The resulting peach tart is at once down-home and exotic.

MAKES 2 SERVINGS

EQUIPMENT

Measuring spoons and measuring cups
Baking sheet
Parchment paper
Vegetable peeler
Paring knife
Cutting board
Medium-size bowl
Spoon
Food processor fitted with metal blade
Strainer or colander

INGREDIENTS

2 large or 3 small ripe peaches
2 tablespoons brandy
½ cup plus 1 tablespoon sugar
⅛ teaspoon 5-spice powder
¼ cup cream cheese, chilled
¼ cup (½ stick) unsalted butter, chilled

½ cup all-purpose flour, plus more for shaping
Pinch of salt

1. Preheat the oven to 400 degrees. Line the baking sheet with parchment paper. Peel the peaches and cut each one in half. Remove the pits. Slice each half into ¼-inch-thick slices. Put the slices in the bowl, add the brandy, ¼ cup of the sugar, and the 5-spice powder. Stir to combine.

2. Place the cream cheese, butter, ½ cup flour, salt, and ¼ cup of the sugar in the work bowl of the food processor. Process just until the dough comes together. It will be sticky. Sprinkle the parchment paper with flour. Turn the dough onto the parchment-lined baking sheet and, with floured hands, press it into a rough 8-inch circle.

3. Give the peaches a stir and then turn them into the strainer to drain the liquid. Arrange about three quarters of the slices in a circle around the border of the dough, overlapping them slightly. Arrange the remaining slices in a smaller inner circle, again slightly overlapping them. Sprinkle the peaches with the remaining 1 tablespoon sugar.

4. Bake until golden, 25 to 30 minutes. Serve warm or at room temperature.

◆

Quickest Pecan Tart

This tart differs from a traditional pecan pie in that it doesn't contain eggs, making it quicker to bake (just 10 minutes) and impossible to curdle. The result is more a confection than a custard pie.

MAKES ONE 9-INCH TART; 6 TO 8 SERVINGS

EQUIPMENT

Measuring spoons and measuring cups
Butter warmer or small saucepan
Medium-size bowl
9-inch tart pan with removable bottom
Medium-size saucepan
Wooden spoon
Wire rack

INGREDIENTS

13 tablespoons unsalted butter
2 tablespoons granulated sugar
1⅓ cups graham cracker crumbs
½ cup firmly packed light brown sugar
¼ cup light corn syrup
2 tablespoons heavy cream
2 cups pecan halves

1. Preheat the oven to 350 degrees. Melt 5 tablespoons of the butter in the butter warmer or saucepan. Combine the granulated sugar and graham cracker crumbs in the bowl and stir in the melted butter. Press the graham cracker mixture evenly across the bottom and all the way up the sides of the tart pan, packing it tightly with your fingertips so it is even and compacted. Place the pan in the freezer until ready to use.

2. Combine the remaining 8 tablespoons butter, the brown sugar, and corn syrup in the medium-size saucepan and bring to a boil, stirring frequently. Boil for 1 minute, stir in the cream and pecans, and boil for another 3 minutes.

3. Pour the hot filling into the tart pan and use the spoon to distribute the nuts evenly across the pan. Bake until the filling is bubbling and slightly browned, about 10 minutes. Cool completely on the rack before removing the sides of the pan and serving.

Maple-Pecan Tart

Just a little more complicated than the previous recipe, this tart should still please pecan lovers who are in a hurry. Maple syrup provides flavor as well as sweetness. Eggs enrich the filling.

MAKES ONE 9-INCH TART; 6 TO 8 SERVINGS

EQUIPMENT

Measuring spoons and measuring cups

Butter warmer or small saucepan

2 medium-size bowls

9-inch tart pan with removable bottom

Wire whisk

Wire rack

INGREDIENTS

½ cup (1 stick) unsalted butter

⅓ cup plus 2 tablespoons sugar

1⅓ cups graham cracker crumbs

¼ cup light corn syrup

2 large eggs

¼ cup pure maple syrup

1½ cups pecan halves

1. Preheat the oven to 325 degrees. Melt 5 tablespoons of the butter in the butter warmer or saucepan. Combine 2 tablespoons of the sugar and the graham cracker crumbs in a medium-size bowl and stir in the melted butter. Press the graham cracker mixture evenly across the bottom and all the way up the sides of the tart pan, packing it tightly with your fingertips so it is even and compacted. Place the pan in the freezer until ready to use.

2. Melt the remaining 3 tablespoons butter. Whisk together the melted butter, the remaining ⅓ cup sugar, the corn syrup, eggs, and maple syrup in the other bowl.

3. Scatter the pecans evenly across the bottom of the tart shell. Slowly pour the filling over the nuts.

4. Bake until the filling is just set, 15 to 20 minutes. Let cool completely on the rack before removing the sides of the pan and serving.

Sourdough Nectarine Tarts

This idea is borrowed from Viana La Place's *Desserts and Sweet Snacks*, a book of very casual but surprisingly satisfying recipes. Leftover slices of sourdough bread are sugared, covered with fruit, and sugared again before being popped in the oven for 12 minutes or so. The stale bread absorbs the juices of the fruit and makes a delightfully chewy crust for the "tart." Peaches or plums may be substituted if you like.

MAKES 4 SERVINGS

EQUIPMENT

Measuring spoons and measuring cups
Paring knife
Cutting board
Butter knife
Baking sheet

INGREDIENTS

2 medium-size ripe nectarines
2 tablespoons unsalted butter, softened
Four ½-inch-thick slices day-old sourdough bread
¼ cup firmly packed light brown sugar

1. Preheat the oven to 450 degrees. Slice each nectarine in half, pit it, and slice each half into four ¼-inch-thick wedges. Butter each slice of bread and sprinkle with ½ tablespoon of the brown sugar. Arrange 4 nectarine wedges on each slice of bread and sprinkle again with ½ tablespoon brown sugar.

2. Place on the baking sheet and bake until the bread is golden and the fruit soft, about 12 minutes. Serve immediately.

Pecan-Caramel-Fudge Pie

I developed this recipe for *Bon Appétit* magazine. The editors wanted something old-fashioned and nostalgic, but lightning-quick to prepare. This confection fits the bill. The crust is made from cookie crumbs and butter (no prebaking) and the pie itself bakes in a mere 10 minutes.

MAKES ONE 9-INCH PIE; 10 SERVINGS

EQUIPMENT

Measuring spoons and measuring cups
Chef's knife
Cutting board
Butter warmer or small saucepan
Food processor fitted with metal blade
Medium-size bowl
Spoon
9-inch pie plate
Medium-size saucepan
Wooden spoon
Wire rack

INGREDIENTS

17 tablespoons unsalted butter
30 Nabisco Famous Chocolate Wafers (to yield about 1⅓ cups crumbs)
⅛ teaspoon salt
¾ cup firmly packed light brown sugar
6 tablespoons light corn syrup

3 tablespoons heavy cream
3 cups pecan halves
2 ounces unsweetened chocolate, finely chopped

1. Preheat the oven to 350 degrees.

2. Melt 5 tablespoons of the butter in the butter warmer or saucepan. Place the cookies in the work bowl of the food processor and process until finely ground. Place the cookie crumbs and salt in the medium-size bowl and stir in the melted butter. Press the mixture evenly across the bottom of the pie plate and all the way up the sides of the pan, packing it tightly with your fingertips so it is even and compacted. Place the pie crust in the freezer until ready to use.

3. Combine the remaining 12 tablespoons butter, the brown sugar, and corn syrup in the medium-size saucepan and bring to a boil,

stirring frequently with a wooden spoon. Boil for 1 minute, stir in the heavy cream and pecans, and boil for another 3 minutes. Remove from the heat, add the chocolate, and stir until completely melted.

4. Pour the hot filling into the pie crust and use the spoon to distribute the nuts evenly across the pan.

5. Bake until the filling is bubbling, about 10 minutes. Let cool completely on the rack before serving.

Peanut Butter Pie

Traditionally, peanut butter pie has a graham cracker crust and a rich fudge topping, but easy as it is, it's difficult to prepare in 15 minutes. I've modified the recipe to make it in the allotted time, and I think I've actually improved it in the process. Instead of an extra-rich cream cheese and peanut butter filling, as is traditional, I use peanut butter mousse. Losing the cream cheese makes the pie lighter and quicker. A chocolate cookie crust eliminates the need for the chocolate topping, although there's certainly no harm in spreading on a thick layer of ganache if you have a few extra minutes (see **5 Minutes Extra**).

MAKES ONE 9-INCH PIE; 10 SERVINGS

EQUIPMENT

Measuring spoons and measuring cups
Butter warmer or small saucepan
Food processor fitted with metal blade
Medium-size bowl
Spoon
9-inch pie plate
Large bowl
Electric mixer fitted with whisk attachment
Small bowl
Rubber spatula

INGREDIENTS

5 tablespoons unsalted butter
30 Nabisco Famous Chocolate Wafers (to yield about 1⅓ cups crumbs)
⅛ teaspoon salt
2 cups heavy cream
¾ cup plus 2 tablespoons confectioners' sugar
2 teaspoons pure vanilla extract
1 cup smooth peanut butter

1. Preheat the oven to 350 degrees. Melt the butter in the butter warmer or saucepan. Place the cookies in the work bowl of the food processor and process until finely ground. Place the cookie crumbs and salt in the medium-size

bowl and stir in the melted butter. Press the mixture evenly across the bottom of the pie plate and all the way up the sides of the pan, packing it tightly with your fingertips so it is even and compacted. Bake until crisp, 6 to 8 minutes. Set aside to cool.

2. Combine the heavy cream, confectioners' sugar, and vanilla in the large bowl and beat with the electric mixer until it holds stiff peaks.

3. Place the peanut butter in the small bowl and stir in one quarter of the whipped cream. Gently fold the lightened peanut butter mixture back into the remaining whipped cream. Scrape the filling into the pie shell, smooth with the spatula, and refrigerate until firm, at least 3 hours.

5 MINUTES EXTRA

It really takes only 5 minutes extra to make the classic fudge topping for this pie. Finely chop 4 ounces bittersweet chocolate and place in a small heatproof bowl. Heat ½ cup heavy cream in a small saucepan or butter warmer until almost boiling. Remove from the heat and whisk in the chocolate until smooth. Cool the topping until just warm to the touch. Spread it over the chilled pie with a rubber spatula. Refrigerate until firm, at least 3 hours or up to 24 hours.

Cocoa Mascarpone and Raspberry Tart with a Chocolate-Almond Crust

Here I press a combination of chocolate cookies and almonds into a pan, fill with cocoa mascarpone, and top with fresh berries. There's no need to carefully place the berries in concentric circles on top of the filling. I like the more natural look of a tart across which the berries have been scattered by the handful (and it's quicker, of course).

MAKES ONE 9-INCH TART; 6 TO 8 SERVINGS

EQUIPMENT

Measuring spoons and measuring cups

Butter knife

Butter warmer or small saucepan

Food processor fitted with metal blade

2 medium-size bowls

Spoon

9-inch tart pan

Nonstick cooking spray

Wire whisk

Metal offset spatula

Fine-mesh strainer

INGREDIENTS

3 tablespoons unsalted butter

½ cup sliced almonds

12 Nabisco Famous Chocolate Wafers (to yield about ½ cup crumbs)

1 cup mascarpone

¼ cup heavy cream

2 teaspoons unsweetened cocoa powder

2 tablespoons confectioners' sugar, plus more for dusting

2 pints fresh raspberries

1. Preheat the oven to 350 degrees. Melt the butter in the butter warmer or saucepan. Place the almonds and cookies in the work bowl of the food processor and grind fine. Place the mixture and the melted butter in one of the bowls. Stir until evenly moistened.

(continued)

2. Spray the tart pan with cooking spray. Press the mixture into the bottom of the pan, but not up the sides. Bake until crisp, 6 to 8 minutes. Set aside to cool.

3. While the tart shell is baking and cooling, whisk together the mascarpone, heavy cream, cocoa powder, and 2 tablespoons confectioners' sugar in the other bowl. Dot the cooled cookie crust with tablespoonfuls of the filling. Smooth the filling over the crust with the spatula, being careful not to stir up the crumbs. Scatter the berries on top of the filling. Refrigerate until ready to serve. The tart can be refrigerated for several hours. Right before serving, sift confectioners' sugar over the berries using the strainer.

White Chocolate–Mint Tart with Strawberries

The contrast of creamy filling, crisp crust, and tart berries makes this simple tart a winner. Whip the white chocolate filling just until it begins to hold soft peaks—a few seconds of overwhipping and it will turn from smooth to grainy. The strawberries may be artfully arranged over the filling, but to save time I spoon them alongside individual slices just before serving.

MAKES ONE 9-INCH TART; 6 TO 8 SERVINGS

EQUIPMENT

Measuring spoons and measuring cups

Butter warmer or small saucepan

Medium-size bowl

2 spoons

9-inch tart pan with removable bottom

Chef's knife

Cutting board

Large bowl

Small saucepan

Wire whisk

Electric mixer fitted with whisk attachment

Rubber spatula

INGREDIENTS

5 tablespoons unsalted butter

2 tablespoons sugar

1⅓ cups graham cracker crumbs

4 ounces white chocolate

1½ cups heavy cream

¼ teaspoon pure mint extract

1 pint fresh strawberries

1. Preheat the oven to 350 degrees. Melt the butter in the butter warmer or saucepan. Combine the sugar and graham cracker crumbs in the medium-size bowl and stir in the melted butter. Press the graham cracker mixture evenly across the bottom and all the way up the sides of the tart pan, packing it tightly with your fingertips so it is even and compacted. Bake

until crisp and golden, 6 to 8 minutes. Set aside to let cool.

2. Finely chop the chocolate and place in a large bowl. Heat the heavy cream in the saucepan until almost boiling. Whisk the hot cream into the chocolate until smooth. Whisk in the mint extract. Refrigerate until completely cooled.

3. Whip the chocolate mixture with the electric mixer until it holds soft peaks. Refrigerate until ready to serve, up to 3 hours. Spoon into the cooled tart shell and smooth with the spatula.

4. To serve, slice the tops off the strawberries and slice thin. Place wedges of the tart on 6 individual dessert dishes and spoon some strawberries alongside each wedge.

Blueberry-Coconut Tart

This tart couldn't be simpler—just mix together eggs, cream, berries, and coconut and spread across a graham cracker crust. Perfect for summer barbecues and picnics.

MAKES ONE 9-INCH TART; 6 SERVINGS

EQUIPMENT

Measuring spoons and measuring cups

Butter knife

Butter warmer or small saucepan

2 medium-size bowls

Spoon

9-inch tart pan with removable bottom

Wire whisk

Wire rack

INGREDIENTS

5 tablespoons unsalted butter

⅓ cup plus 2 tablespoons sugar

1⅓ cups graham cracker crumbs

2 large eggs

½ cup heavy cream

1 pint fresh blueberries, picked over for stems

1¼ cups sweetened flaked coconut

1. Preheat the oven to 350 degrees. Melt the butter in the butter warmer or saucepan. Combine 2 tablespoons of the sugar and the graham cracker crumbs in one of the bowls and stir in the melted butter. Press the graham cracker mixture evenly across the bottom and all the way up the sides of the the pan, packing it tightly with your fingertips so it is even and compacted.

2. Whisk together the remaining ⅓ cup sugar, the eggs, and heavy cream in the other bowl. Stir in the blueberries and coconut gently to combine.

3. Spoon the filling into the tart pan. Bake until the berry mixture is bubbling and slightly browned, 45 to 50 minutes. Let cool completely on the rack before removing the sides of the pan and serving.

Oat-Crisped Pears with Sour Cream

It's not always necessary to make a pie crust to get your pie fix. For this simple dessert, pear wedges are coated with a mixture of sugar, spices, and oats for a crispy crust without the pie.

MAKES 4 SERVINGS

EQUIPMENT

Measuring cups and measuring spoons
Baking sheet
Parchment paper
Vegetable peeler
Cutting board
Paring knife
Food processor fitted with metal blade
3 small bowls
Wire whisk

INGREDIENTS

4 ripe but firm pears
½ cup rolled (old-fashioned) oats
¼ cup whole almonds
¼ cup firmly packed dark brown sugar
¼ teaspoon ground cinnamon
¼ teaspoon ground ginger
1 large egg
¾ cup sour cream
2 tablespoons confectioners' sugar

1. Preheat the oven to 350 degrees. Line the baking sheet with a piece of parchment paper.

2. Peel the pears and cut into quarters. Cut away the core from each quarter.

3. Combine the oats, almonds, brown sugar, cinnamon, and ginger in the work bowl of the food processor and process until the almonds are coarsely chopped. Transfer to one of the bowls.

4. Lightly beat the egg in another of the bowls. Dip each pear wedge first in the beaten egg and then roll in the oat mixture to coat. Place on the prepared baking sheet. Bake the pear wedges until soft and golden, 20 to 25 minutes. While the pears are baking, whisk together the sour cream and confectioners' sugar in the last bowl. Let the pears cool on the baking sheet for 5 minutes and serve warm with the sweetened sour cream.

Strawberry Cobbler with a Lemon Butter Cookie Crust

This is just cookie dough spooned over berries and baked until golden. No need to carefully hull the berries; it's quicker to simply slice off the stems. This cobbler is best served warm. If you'd like to make it ahead of time, reheat in a 350-degree oven for 15 minutes before serving.

MAKES 6 SERVINGS

EQUIPMENT

Measuring cups and measuring spoons

Citrus zester

Cutting board

Paring knife

Large bowl

Spoon

Medium-size bowl

Electric mixer fitted with paddle attachment

Rubber spatula

8-inch square baking dish

Wire rack

INGREDIENTS

2 pints fresh strawberries

3/4 cup sugar

1 tablespoon cornstarch

1/2 cup (1 stick) unsalted butter, softened

1 large egg yolk

1/2 teaspoon pure vanilla extract

1 teaspoon grated lemon zest

1/2 cup all-purpose flour

1/4 teaspoon baking powder

Pinch of salt

1 pint vanilla ice cream, softened a bit

1. Preheat the oven to 375 degrees.

2. Wash the strawberries and trim off the stems (no need to hull them). If large, cut in half; if small, leave whole. Combine the strawberries,

¼ cup of the sugar, and the cornstarch in the large bowl. Let stand, stirring occasionally, until the sugar dissolves, 5 to 7 minutes.

3. While the berries are standing, make the crust. Cream together the butter and remaining ½ cup sugar in the medium-size bowl with the electric mixer until smooth. Beat in the egg yolk, vanilla, and lemon zest until smooth, scraping down the sides of the bowl with the spatula as necessary. Add the flour, baking powder, and salt and stir until just combined.

4. Spoon the strawberries into the baking dish. Drop the dough in rounded tablespoonfuls over the fruit. Bake until the fruit is bubbling and the crust is golden, 50 to 55 minutes. Let cool slightly and serve warm, with the ice cream.

Pear and Cornmeal Cobbler

It's amazing how the addition of 1 ingredient can transform a basic recipe. Cornmeal gives this cobbler topping an appealingly crunchy texture, harmonizing beautifully with the meltingly soft pears.

MAKES 6 SERVINGS

EQUIPMENT

Measuring cups and measuring spoons

Vegetable peeler

Cutting board

Paring knife

Large bowl

Medium-size bowl

Electric mixer fitted with paddle attachment

Rubber spatula

Tablespoon

8-inch square baking dish

INGREDIENTS

2 pounds ripe pears

½ cup sugar

2 teaspoons cornstarch

½ cup (1 stick) unsalted butter, softened

1 large egg yolk

½ teaspoon pure vanilla extract

½ cup all-purpose flour

¼ cup cornmeal

¼ teaspoon baking powder

Pinch of salt

1 pint vanilla ice cream, softened a bit

1. Preheat the oven to 375 degrees.

2. Peel, halve, and core the pears. Slice each half into 3 or 4 wedges. Combine the pears, ¼ cup of the sugar, and the cornstarch in a large bowl. Let stand, stirring occasionally, until the sugar dissolves, 5 to 7 minutes.

3. While the pears are standing, make the crust. Cream together the butter and remaining ¼ cup sugar in the medium-size bowl with the electric mixer until smooth. Beat in the egg yolk and vanilla until smooth, scraping down the sides of the bowl as necessary with the spatula. Add the flour, cornmeal, baking powder, and salt and stir just until combined.

(continued)

4. Spoon the pears into the baking dish. Drop the topping in rounded tablespoonsful over the fruit. Bake until the fruit is bubbling and the crust is golden, 50 to 55 minutes. Let cool slightly and serve warm, with the ice cream. ◆

Blueberry-Walnut Crisp

This is my basic crisp topping—walnuts, brown sugar, flour, butter—sprinkled
over blueberries. Any other fruit may be substituted (apples, pears, peaches,
and plums are all good), but few are quicker to prepare than blueberries,
which just need to be washed and picked over.

MAKES 6 SERVINGS

EQUIPMENT

Measuring cups and measuring spoons

8-inch square baking dish

Wooden spoon

Chef's knife

Cutting board

Small bowl

Electric mixer fitted with paddle attachment

INGREDIENTS

2 pints fresh blueberries, picked over for stems

*1/3 cup plus 2 tablespoons firmly packed light brown
   sugar*

1 tablespoon cornstarch

1/4 cup walnuts

1/2 cup all-purpose flour

1/8 teaspoon ground cinnamon

Pinch of salt

*1/4 cup (1/2 stick) unsalted butter, chilled and cut into
   small pieces*

1 pint vanilla ice cream, softened a bit

1. Preheat the oven to 425 degrees. Combine
the blueberries, 1/3 cup of the brown sugar, and
the cornstarch in the baking pan. Stir to
combine, mashing some, but not all, of the
berries with the back of the spoon to release
some of the juices. Stir once or twice while
preparing the topping.

2. Coarsely chop the walnuts. Combine the
nuts, flour, remaining 2 tablespoons brown
sugar, the cinnamon, and salt in the small bowl
and mix for several seconds to combine. Add
the butter and mix on low speed with the
electric mixer just until clumps begin to form,
1 to 2 minutes. Do not overmix.

3. Scatter the topping over the fruit and bake
until golden and bubbling, about 30 minutes.
Serve warm with ice cream on the side.

Peach-Cardamom Crumble

A dash of cardamom adds an intriguing note to this simplest
of fruit-and-pastry desserts.

MAKES 6 SERVINGS

EQUIPMENT

Measuring spoons and measuring cups

Cutting board

Paring knife

Large bowl

Spoon

Food processor fitted with metal blade

8-inch square baking dish

INGREDIENTS

1¾ pounds ripe but firm peaches (6 or 7 medium-
size peaches)

¼ teaspoon ground cardamom

½ cup plus 1 tablespoon sugar

1 tablespoon cornstarch

1 cup all-purpose flour

6 tablespoons (¾ stick) unsalted butter, chilled

Sweetened whipped cream for garnish (optional)

1. Preheat the oven to 425 degrees.

2. Halve and pit the peaches. Cut each half into
4 wedges. Combine the peaches, cardamom,
½ cup sugar, and the cornstarch in the bowl.
Let stand, stirring occasionally, until the sugar
dissolves, 5 to 7 minutes.

3. While the peaches are standing, make the
topping. Combine the flour, butter, and the
remaining 1 tablespoon sugar in the work bowl
of the food processor. Process until the mixture
has the texture of bread crumbs.

4. Transfer the peaches to the baking dish.
Scatter the topping over the fruit. Bake until
the fruit is bubbling and the crust is golden,
35 to 40 minutes. Let cool slightly and serve
warm, with sweetened whipped cream if
desired.

Raspberry Brownie Cobbler

Here is a dessert for people who have trouble deciding between fruit and chocolate—raspberries topped with chocolate-nut batter rather than the usual oats or crumbs. It's best served warm, so pop it in the oven a little before you sit down to dinner and serve about an hour later, with vanilla ice cream if you like.

MAKES 6 TO 8 SERVINGS

EQUIPMENT

Measuring cups and measuring spoons

Medium-size saucepan and medium-size stainless
    steel bowl or double boiler

Wire whisk

Chef's knife

Cutting board

8-inch square baking dish

Nonstick cooking spray

Medium-size bowl

2 spoons

Rubber spatula

Toothpick

INGREDIENTS

2½ ounces bittersweet chocolate

½ cup (1 stick) unsalted butter, cut into several
    pieces

½ cup walnuts

1 pint fresh raspberries

1 cup sugar

2 large eggs

½ teaspoon pure vanilla extract

7 tablespoons all-purpose flour

¼ teaspoon salt

1 pint vanilla ice cream, softened a bit
    (optional)

1. Preheat the oven to 350 degrees. Put 2 inches of water in the saucepan or the bottom of the double boiler and bring to a bare simmer. Combine the chocolate and butter in the stainless steel bowl and place it on top of the simmering water, making sure that the water doesn't touch the bowl. Heat, whisking occasionally, until the chocolate and butter are completely melted.

2. While the chocolate is melting, coarsely chop the nuts. Spray the baking dish with cooking

spray. Scatter the berries across the bottom of the dish.

3. Whisk together the sugar, eggs, and vanilla in the bowl. Whisk in the melted chocolate. Stir in the flour, nuts, and salt. Pour the batter over the berries and smooth with the spatula.

4. Bake until a toothpick inserted into the center of the cobbler comes out clean, about 45 minutes. Let stand for 15 minutes and serve with ice cream if desired.

Plum Brown Betty

White bread provides a satisfyingly crunchy contrast to soft fruit in this
easy classic. The topping is rather spare, so the vanilla ice cream
adds an element of luxury.

MAKES 6 SERVINGS

EQUIPMENT

Measuring cups and measuring spoons
Cutting board
Paring knife
Medium-size bowl
Spoon
Butter warmer or small saucepan
Food processor fitted with metal blade
Small bowl
8-inch square baking dish

INGREDIENTS

1¾ pounds ripe but firm plums (about 9 plums)
⅔ cup firmly packed dark brown sugar
1 tablespoon cornstarch
¼ cup (½ stick) unsalted butter
4 slices firm white sandwich bread (about 4 ounces)
¼ teaspoon ground cinnamon
1 pint vanilla ice cream, softened a bit

1. Preheat the oven to 375 degrees. Halve and
pit the plums. Slice each half into thirds.
Combine the plums, ⅓ cup of the brown sugar,
and the cornstarch in the medium-size bowl.
Stir once or twice while preparing the topping.

2. Melt 3 tablespoons of the butter in the butter
warmer or saucepan. Tear the bread into large
pieces, place in the work bowl of the food
processor, and process into coarse crumbs.
Transfer to the small bowl and toss with the
melted butter, the remaining ⅓ cup brown
sugar, and the cinnamon.

3. Transfer the plums to the baking dish. Scatter
the topping over the fruit. Cut the remaining
tablespoon butter into small pieces and scatter
over the topping. Bake until golden and
bubbling, 40 to 45 minutes. Serve warm with
the ice cream on the side.

MAKING YOUR OWN QUICK PUFF PASTRY

*Quick homemade puff pastry, mixed in a food processor, can be made in less than
15 minutes. If you'd like to try it, here's a recipe adapted from Nick Malgieri's great book* How
to Bake. *While classic puff pastry is rolled out and folded many times to create
the layers that puff, Nick's quick puff pastry is rolled out only once, folded, and then
rolled into a tight cylinder to create layers without all the repeat rolling and folding.
For extra-tender pastry, substitute ¼ cup cake flour for ¼ cup of the all-purpose flour. This
recipe makes about 1 pound of pastry. Use a half pound for any of the recipes
in this chapter and freeze the other half for later use.*

EQUIPMENT

Measuring cups and measuring spoons
Butter knife
Cutting board
Food processor fitted with metal blade
Rolling pin
Plastic wrap

INGREDIENTS

*1½ cups all-purpose flour, plus more
    for dusting*
¾ teaspoon salt
*15 tablespoons unsalted butter, chilled and cut into
    small pieces*
6 tablespoons ice water

1. Combine the 1½ cups flour and the salt in the work bowl of the food processor. Pulse to combine.

2. Add the butter to the work bowl. Pulse once or twice to combine. Add the water and pulse until the ingredients form a rough ball. Do not overprocess.

3. Flour your work surface. Shape the dough into a rough rectangle and roll out so that it measures 8 × 12 inches. Lift the dough from the work surface frequently and sprinkle with flour to make sure that it doesn't stick.

4. Fold the rectangle into thirds, as if it were a letter. Starting at one short end, tightly roll up the folded pastry so that you have a short, thick cylinder. Press the cylinder into a 4 × 6-inch rectangle. Cover with plastic wrap and refrigerate overnight or up to 3 days before using. Puff pastry can be frozen for up to 2 weeks and thawed in the refrigerator before using.

Bittersweet Chocolate Turnovers

Frozen puff pastry is one of my favorite ingredients. All-butter brands such as Dufour are as good if not better than pastry you could make yourself, and are used in the finest bakeries and restaurants (avoid puff pastry made with shortening—it just doesn't have the same flavor). Although puff pastry turnovers are very quick to prepare, there is a little bit of time involved in getting the pastry to the right temperature. First, it has to be thawed so that it is workable (about 15 minutes). Then it has to be chilled again before baking. Puff pastry that is too warm and soft will melt, rather than puff, in the oven, so the filled turnovers need to be frozen for at least 15 minutes before being placed in the hot oven. Turnovers can be prepared, covered in plastic wrap, and frozen for 2 weeks. No need to thaw them out—just place in the preheated oven and bake until puffed and golden.

MAKES 4 TURNOVERS

EQUIPMENT

Chef's knife
Cutting board
Fork
Small bowl
Rolling pin
Paring knife
Pastry brush
Baking sheet
Spatula
Wire rack
Fine-mesh strainer

INGREDIENTS

1 large egg
All-purpose flour for dusting
1 sheet (about ½ pound) frozen puff pastry, thawed
3 ounces bittersweet chocolate, cut into small pieces
Confectioners' sugar for dusting

1. Preheat the oven to 425 degrees. Lightly beat the egg in the bowl. Dust your work surface with flour. Unfold the puff pastry and roll it out into a 12-inch square. Cut into four 6-inch squares. Place some chocolate just below the center of each square. Brush the edges of the square with the beaten egg. Fold over to make a triangle. Use the tines of the fork to crimp the edges shut. Freeze for at least 15 minutes or cover with plastic wrap and freeze up to 2 weeks.

2. When ready to bake, brush the tops of the turnovers with the egg. Cut three ½-inch slits on the top of each turnover to allow the steam to escape.

3. Transfer the turnovers to the baking sheet and bake until puffed and golden, 12 to 14 minutes (turnovers that have been completely frozen may take a few minutes longer). Transfer the baking sheet to the wire rack, let cool for 10 minutes, dust with confectioners' sugar using the strainer, and serve warm. (Turnovers may be made several hours in advance and reheated for 8 minutes in a preheated 350-degree oven before serving.)

Raspberry-Cheese Turnovers

Depending on your mood, these could be either a simple dessert or a
decadent breakfast. If you'd like them in the morning, prepare the night
before and freeze. Put the frozen turnovers in the oven and you'll have
a bakery breakfast in minutes.

MAKES 4 TURNOVERS

EQUIPMENT

Measuring cups and measuring spoons
Paring knife
2 small bowls
2 forks
Rolling pin
Pastry brush
Baking sheet
Spatula
Wire rack
Fine-mesh strainer

INGREDIENTS

4 ounces cream cheese, softened
½ cup fresh raspberries
3 tablespoons firmly packed light brown sugar
1 large egg
All-purpose flour for dusting
1 sheet (about ½ pound) frozen puff pastry, thawed
Confectioners' sugar for dusting

1. Preheat the oven to 425 degrees.

2. Cut the cream cheese into small pieces and
combine in one of the bowls with the berries
and brown sugar. Mash together with the fork.

3. Lightly beat the egg in the other bowl. Dust
your work surface with flour. Unfold the puff
pastry and roll it out into a 12-inch square. Cut
into four 6-inch squares with the knife. Place
2 tablespoons of the filling in the center of each
square. Brush the edges with the beaten egg.
Fold over to make a triangle. Use the tines of
the fork to crimp the edges shut. Freeze for at
least 15 minutes or cover with plastic wrap and
freeze up to 2 weeks. Brush the tops of the
turnovers with the beaten egg. Cut three
½-inch slits on the top of each turnover to
allow the steam to escape.

(continued)

4. Transfer the turnovers to the baking sheet and bake until puffed and golden, 12 to 14 minutes (turnovers that have been completely frozen may take a few minutes longer). Transfer the baking sheet to the wire rack. Let cool for 10 minutes, dust with confectioners' sugar using the strainer, and serve warm. (Turnovers may be made several hours in advance and reheated for 8 minutes in a preheated 350-degree oven before serving.)

Apricot and White Chocolate Turnovers

I like the tartness of apricot jam in contrast to the sweetness of the chocolate, but any favorite jam may be substituted.

MAKES 4 TURNOVERS

EQUIPMENT

Measuring spoons
Chef's knife
Cutting board
Small bowl
Fork
Rolling pin
Paring knife
Pastry brush
Baking sheet
Spatula
Wire rack

INGREDIENTS

1 large egg
All-purpose flour for dusting
1 sheet (about ½ pound) frozen puff pastry, thawed
3 ounces white chocolate, cut into small pieces
6 tablespoons apricot jam
1 tablespoon sugar

1. Preheat the oven to 425 degrees.

2. Lightly beat the egg in the bowl. Dust your work surface with flour. Unfold the puff pastry and roll it out into a 12-inch square. Cut it into four 6-inch squares with the paring knife. Place some chocolate just below the center of each square. Place 1½ tablespoons of the jam on top of the chocolate. Brush the edges of the pastry with the beaten egg. Fold over to make a triangle. Use the tines of the fork to crimp the edges shut. Freeze for at least 15 minutes or cover with plastic wrap and freeze up to 2 weeks.

3. Remove from the freezer and brush the tops of the turnovers with the beaten egg. Cut three ½-inch slits in the top of each turnover to allow the steam to escape. Sprinkle them with the sugar.

(continued)

4. Transfer the turnovers to the baking sheet and bake until puffed and golden, 12 to 14 minutes (turnovers that have been completely frozen may take a few minutes longer). Transfer the baking sheet to the wire rack. Let cool for 10 minutes and serve warm. (Turnovers may be made several hours in advance and reheated for 8 minutes in a preheated 350-degree oven before serving.)

Puff Pastry Apple Tartlets

The aroma and flavor of these tartlets will transport you. Make sure to slice your apples thinly, since they are not precooked before baking.

MAKES 4 TARTLETS

EQUIPMENT

Measuring spoons
Cutting board
Paring knife
Medium-size bowl
Rolling pin
Baking sheet
Small bowl
Pastry brush
Spatula
Fine-mesh strainer
Wire rack

INGREDIENTS

2 small tart apples, like Granny Smith
1 tablespoon fresh lemon juice
2 tablespoons granulated sugar
All-purpose flour for dusting
1 large egg
1 sheet (about ½ pound) frozen puff pastry, thawed
Confectioners' sugar for dusting

1. Preheat the oven to 425 degrees.

2. Peel, core, and slice the apples ⅛ inch thick. Place the apples in the medium-size bowl and toss with the lemon juice and granulated sugar.

3. Dust the work surface with flour. Unfold the puff pastry and roll it out into a 12-inch square. Cut into four 6-inch squares. Place some apples in the center of each square. Fold the corners in so that they just touch in the center. Place on a baking sheet and refrigerate for 15 minutes.

4. Lightly beat the egg in the small bowl, brush the tartlets with the egg, and bake until puffed and golden, 15 to 18 minutes. Transfer the baking sheet to the rack. Let cool for 10 minutes, dust with confectioners' sugar using the strainer, and serve warm.

(Tartlets may be made several hours in advance and reheated for 8 minutes in a preheated 350-degree oven before serving.)

CHOCOLATE-BUTTERMILK SNACKING CAKE

EASIEST, BEST CHOCOLATE MOUSSE CAKE

FLOURLESS CHOCOLATE-ALMOND CAKE

VANILLA BEAN CHEESECAKE

RICOTTA CHEESECAKE

WARM GINGERBREAD SQUARES

SOUR CREAM–PECAN COFFEE CAKE

OLIVE OIL AND ORANGE CAKE

SIMPLE PINE NUT CAKE

PECAN-BOURBON CAKE

APRICOT-ALMOND CAKE

BUTTERMILK-CORNMEAL CAKE WITH BERRIES AND CREAM

ALMOND-SCENTED CREAM CAKE

PUMPKIN-SPICE POUND CAKE

GOLDEN HONEY POUND CAKE

LEMON CREAM CUPCAKES

VANILLA BEAN CUPCAKES

INDIVIDUAL MOLTEN CHOCOLATE CAKES

OATMEAL SHORTCAKES WITH RASPBERRIES AND CREAM

CAKE WASN'T THE FIRST THING THAT CAME TO MY MIND when I began to think about quick desserts. Bakery varieties almost always consist of several components—cake, filling, frosting, decorations—beyond the reach of cooks with only fifteen minutes to spare. I've made my share of elaborate celebration cakes, put together over the course of several days, but I've also made quite a lot of gingerbread squares and vanilla bean cupcakes as after-school or after-dinner treats. When I started to think of cake in these terms, quick cake started to make sense.

Plain homemade cakes, without the frills, are almost as easy to make as the kind that come out of the box. Many can be stirred together in 1 bowl or whirled together in the work bowl of a food processor. Of course, without thick layers of buttercream or piped roses as distractions, the cake itself must taste great. To keep cakes simple yet sensational, I try to choose just a few quality ingredients that deliver knockout flavor. What they lack in complexity, plain cakes should make up for in straightforward goodness.

I immediately thought of flourless cakes when I began to put this chapter together. After all, by definition they already contain 1 less ingredient than you might expect when approaching a cake recipe. Two universal favorites, cheesecake and chocolate cake, turn out to be simple to prepare. The first recipe in the chapter, Vanilla Bean Cheesecake, doesn't even need to be baked. Seeds from a vanilla bean give it true, pure flavor. The most difficult thing about making the Easiest, Best Chocolate Mousse Cake is carefully placing it in a water bath in the oven. The cake contains only 3 ingredients, stirred together and poured into a springform pan. If one of those ingredients is best-quality bittersweet chocolate and the other two are butter and eggs, how can you go wrong?

Next on my list were "snacking cakes" that could be cut into squares and eaten out of hand soon after being pulled from the oven. I have yet to find a better example than Chocolate-

Buttermilk Snacking Cake, versions of which appear in almost every classic cookbook from *Fannie Farmer* to *The Joy of Cooking*. Top-quality cocoa powder and cake flour give my version a pure chocolate flavor and surprisingly refined texture. The crumb topping and the batter for Sour Cream–Pecan Coffee Cake are mixed in the same food processor work bowl, making the cake quick to prepare even though it has two components. Like all the best coffee cakes, it gets its moist texture from sour cream and its rich flavor from brown sugar in both the batter and the crumbs.

Cakes baked in round pans, plain though they may be, are easily dressed up for dinner guests. Two favorites in this category rely on whipped cream and/or berries for finishing. Buttermilk-Cornmeal Cake with Berries and Cream is mixed in a food processor in mere seconds. It bakes up golden and slightly crunchy, providing a delightful contrast to sweet berries and whipped cream. Preparation of Almond-Scented Cream Cake is extra-quick because there's no butter to incorporate into the batter, just heavy cream to give the cake a little moisture. With juicy sliced strawberries on the side, it is a worthy end to a casual dinner for friends.

Two varieties of buttery pound cake, Pumpkin-Spice and Golden Honey, are easy enough to qualify as everyday treats but unusual enough to merit serving when company comes over. Pumpkin-Spice Pound Cake, made with pumpkin puree, is incredibly moist. With a scoop of ginger-flavored mascarpone, it makes a comforting but unusual and special dessert. Golden Honey Pound Cake has a deep golden color and flowery aroma. It's terrific plain, but I also like to serve lightly toasted slices with small scoops of chocolate and vanilla ice cream. Both cakes, by the way, are mixed in the food processor; preparing the batter for the oven, then, is simply a matter of organizing your ingredients and systematically adding them to the work bowl.

The cupcake recipes here are just as quick to mix as the preceding cakes, and take less than half the time to bake. Each is special in its own way. Lemon Cream Cupcakes have delightfully surprising cream cheese centers. Individual Molten Chocolate Cakes are less like cupcakes than individual soufflés, easy enough to whip up after a weeknight dinner and impressive enough to serve after an elaborate meal for guests.

Fruit shortcakes are an essential part of any baker's repertoire but, simple as they are, they can be time-consuming. The recipe I include here, for Oatmeal Shortcakes with Raspberries and Cream, pushes the 15-minute limit, since it has 3 components that must be prepared separately. But with organization it can be done. The shortcakes don't need to be rolled, just dropped in mounds and baked. Using raspberries means that you don't have to peel or slice the fruit—just mix with sugar a little ahead of time and then spoon onto the biscuit. There should be enough time left over to whip some cream to finish things off.

Other recipes that are a piece of cake:

Amazing Almost Instant Warm Brownies and Ice Cream (page 20)

Mini Peanut Butter Cups (page 24)

Brown Sugar Mini Cupcakes (page 25)

Nut Butter Blondies (page 184)

Chocolate-Buttermilk Snacking Cake

Melting the butter saves time in this traditional no-egg chocolate cake recipe.
Use a high-quality cocoa powder (I swear by Pernigotti), since the flavor
relies on this ingredient. Cake flour gives the cake a finer crumb, but use
all-purpose if it's all you have on hand.

MAKES 8 SQUARES

EQUIPMENT

Measuring cups and measuring spoons
8-inch square baking pan
Nonstick cooking spray
Butter warmer or small saucepan
Large bowl
Electric mixer fitted with paddle attachment
Rubber spatula
Toothpick
2 wire racks

INGREDIENTS

½ cup (1 stick) unsalted butter
1¾ cups cake flour or all-purpose flour
¾ cup unsweetened cocoa powder
1 cup sugar
1 teaspoon baking soda
¼ teaspoon salt
1 cup buttermilk
2 teaspoons pure vanilla extract

1. Preheat the oven to 350 degrees. Spray the baking pan with cooking spray. Melt the butter in the butter warmer or saucepan and set aside to cool slightly.

2. Combine the flour, cocoa, sugar, baking soda, and salt in the bowl. Add the buttermilk, vanilla, and melted butter and beat with the mixer on medium-low speed until combined, about 1 minute.

3. Scrape the batter into the prepared pan with the spatula and bake until the toothpick inserted into the center comes out clean, about 35 minutes. Let cool in the pan about 10 minutes, invert onto a wire rack, and then reinvert on another rack to cool completely. Slice into squares to serve.

Easiest, Best Chocolate Mousse Cake

With only 3 ingredients, cake doesn't get any easier. And when the 3 ingredients are eggs, chocolate, and butter, the cake is a killer. Semisweet chocolate may be used here, but bittersweet will make the most intensely flavored cake.

MAKES ONE 8-INCH CAKE; 12 SERVINGS

EQUIPMENT

Roasting pan

8-inch springform pan

Parchment paper

Nonstick cooking spray

Heavy-duty aluminum foil

Double boiler or medium-size saucepan and
    medium-size stainless steel bowl

Chef's knife

Cutting board

Large bowl

Wire whisk

Spatula

Wire rack

Plastic wrap

Waxed paper

Serving platter

INGREDIENTS

1 pound bittersweet chocolate

1 cup (2 sticks) unsalted butter

8 large eggs

1. Preheat the oven to 350 degrees. Place the roasting pan in the oven and pour in ½ inch of hot water. Line the bottom of the springform pan with parchment paper and spray with cooking spray. Place the pan on a sheet of aluminum foil and mold the foil to the sides, but not over the top, of the pan to prevent water from seeping in.

2. Put 1 inch of water in the bottom of the double boiler or saucepan and bring to a bare simmer over medium-low heat. Finely chop the chocolate. Combine the chocolate and butter in the top of the double boiler or in the steel bowl

and place it on top of the simmering water, making sure that the water doesn't touch the double-boiler top or the bowl. Heat, whisking occasionally, until the chocolate is completely melted. Set aside to cool until barely warm.

3. Break the eggs into the large bowl and whisk to break up. Slowly whisk the eggs into the chocolate mixture until well combined. Scrape the batter into the prepared pan.

4. Carefully place the pan into the roasting pan of hot water and bake until set around the edges but still loose in the center, about 30 minutes. Carefully lift the pan from the water and let cool on the wire rack. Cover with plastic wrap and refrigerate overnight. To serve, remove the springform pan sides, invert the cake onto a sheet of waxed paper, peel off the parchment, and reinvert the cake onto a serving platter, discarding the waxed paper.

Flourless Chocolate-Almond Cake

This is more of a nut cake, flavored with a little chocolate, than a decadent flourless chocolate cake. Skinned hazelnuts may be substituted for the almonds if you like. Although I developed this recipe because I love nuts and chocolate together, I've found it to be a very popular Passover cake. I no longer fuss with matzoh meal and vegetable oil concoctions now that I have this simply perfect recipe.

MAKES ONE 8-INCH CAKE; 12 SERVINGS

EQUIPMENT

Measuring cups

8-inch springform pan

Nonstick cooking spray

Double boiler or medium-size saucepan and
    medium-size stainless steel bowl

Chef's knife

Cutting board

Food processor fitted with metal blade

2 large bowls

Wire whisk

Electric mixer fitted with whisk attachment

Rubber spatula

Wire rack

INGREDIENTS

5 ounces bittersweet chocolate

1⅔ cups whole almonds

8 large eggs

¾ cup sugar

1. Preheat the oven to 350 degrees. Spray the springform pan with cooking spray.

2. Put 1 inch of water into the bottom of the double boiler or saucepan and bring to a bare simmer over medium-low heat. Finely chop the chocolate. Place the chocolate in the top of the double boiler or in the steel bowl and set it over the simmering water, making sure that the water doesn't touch the double-boiler top or the bowl. Heat, whisking occasionally, until the chocolate is completely melted. Set aside to cool until barely warm.

3. While the chocolate is melting, place the almonds in the work bowl of the food processor and pulse several times until finely chopped (but not ground).

4. Separate the eggs, placing the whites in one of the bowls and the yolks in the other bowl. Whisk the chocolate, almonds, and sugar into the yolks. Beat the whites with the mixer on high speed until they hold stiff peaks. Gently fold the whites into the yolk mixture until no more white is visible.

5. Scrape the batter into the prepared pan with the spatula. Bake until risen and the center springs back when lightly touched, about 50 minutes. Let cool on the wire rack completely before removing the sides of the pan and serving.

◆

Vanilla Bean Cheesecake

This small no-bake cheesecake is particularly simple because it doesn't have any crust. The vanilla bean gives it a rich and sophisticated flavor.

MAKES ONE 6-INCH CAKE; 6 SERVINGS

EQUIPMENT

Measuring cups and measuring spoons
Small stainless steel bowl
6-inch spingform pan
Nonstick cooking spray
Small saucepan
Spoon
Paring knife
Zippered-top plastic bag
Large bowl
Electric mixer fitted with paddle attachment
Rubber spatula
Plastic wrap

INGREDIENTS

2 tablespoons water
½ teaspoon unflavored gelatin
1 vanilla bean
Two 8-ounce packages cream cheese, at room temperature
6 tablespoons heavy cream
⅔ cup sugar

1. Place the water in the bowl and sprinkle with the gelatin. Let stand to dissolve, 2 to 3 minutes. Spray the springform pan with cooking spray. Place 1 inch of water in the saucepan and bring to a bare simmer over medium-low heat. Place the bowl on top of the saucepan and stir until the gelatin mixture is smooth, 1 to 2 minutes. Do not overheat.

2. With the knife, split the vanilla bean in half lengthwise. Place one half in the plastic bag and reserve for another use. Scrape the seeds from the other half into the large bowl and add the cream cheese, heavy cream, and sugar. Beat with the mixer until light and fluffy, scraping down the sides of the bowl once or twice, 2 to 3 minutes. Beat in the gelatin mixture. Scrape the cheesecake batter into the prepared pan and smooth the top with the spatula. Cover with plastic wrap and refrigerate until firm, at least 6 hours or overnight. To unmold, run the paring

knife around the edge of the pan and release the sides of the pan.

5 MINUTES EXTRA

Fifteen minutes before serving, cut the stems off 1 pint fresh strawberries and thinly slice. Place in a medium-size bowl with 3 tablespoons sugar, 3 tablespoons dark rum, and the seeds from the other half of the vanilla bean. Toss to combine and toss once or twice more to dissolve the sugar. Serve slices of the cheesecake with the macerated berries.

Ricotta Cheesecake

This no-crust cheesecake has a light texture and rich, eggy flavor. It will rise like a soufflé in the oven and then fall during the last 10 minutes or so of baking. To save time, I utilize both the food processor and the electric mixer—a little extra cleanup, but I'm able to whip the egg whites and mix the batter without washing and drying the bowl of my mixer during preparation.

MAKES ONE 9-INCH CAKE; 8 TO 10 SERVINGS

EQUIPMENT

Measuring cups and measuring spoons
Citrus zester
9-inch springform pan
Nonstick cooking spray
Rubber spatula
2 large bowls
Food processor fitted with metal blade
Electric mixer fitted with whisk attachment
Wire rack
Plastic wrap
Fine-mesh strainer

INGREDIENTS

6 large eggs
⅔ cup sugar
2 teaspoons pure vanilla extract
Two 15-ounce containers whole-milk ricotta cheese

2 teaspoons grated lemon zest
Confectioners' sugar for dusting

1. Preheat the oven to 325 degrees. Spray the springform pan with cooking spray. Separate the eggs, placing the whites in one of the large bowls and the yolks in the work bowl of a food processor.

2. Add the sugar and vanilla to the work bowl of the food processor and process until thick and light yellow, about 1 minute. Add the ricotta and zest and process until smooth, another 30 seconds. Scrape the mixture into the other large bowl.

3. Beat the whites on high speed with the mixer until they hold stiff peaks. Fold the whites into

the ricotta mixture and scrape into the prepared pan, smoothing the top with the spatula.

4. Bake until the cake is deep golden brown and the sides begin to pull away from the pan, about 1 hour and 20 minutes. Transfer to the rack to let cool completely. Cover with plastic wrap and refrigerate until serving, at least 6 hours and up to 1 day. To serve, release the sides of the springform pan, dust with confectioners' sugar using the strainer, and cut into wedges.

Warm Gingerbread Squares

This is one of my all-time favorite recipes. The texture of the cake is light and airy, but the flavor is all deep, dark molasses and spices. It's very good at room temperature, but why wait until it's completely cooled?

MAKES 8 SQUARES

EQUIPMENT

Measuring cups and measuring spoons

Butter knife

8-inch square baking pan

Nonstick cooking spray

Small saucepan

Spoon

Food processor fitted with metal blade

Rubber spatula

Toothpick

INGREDIENTS

3/4 cup water

1/2 cup dark molasses

1 teaspoon baking soda

1/4 cup (1/2 stick) unsalted butter, softened

1/2 cup firmly packed light brown sugar

1 large egg yolk

1/4 teaspoon salt

1 1/2 teaspoons ground ginger

1/2 teaspoon ground cinnamon

1 teaspoon baking powder

1 1/4 cups all-purpose flour

1. Preheat the oven to 350 degrees. Spray the baking pan with cooking spray.

2. Bring the water to a boil in the saucepan. Stir in the molasses and baking soda and remove from the heat. Set aside to let cool slightly.

3. Combine the butter and brown sugar in the work bowl of the food processor and process until smooth, scraping down the sides of the bowl once or twice as necessary. Add the egg yolk and process until smooth, scraping down the sides of the bowl as necessary. Pour the molasses mixture through the feed tube and pulse once or twice to incorporate. Add the salt, ginger, cinnamon, baking powder, and flour and pulse once or twice to incorporate.

4. Scrape the batter into the prepared pan with the spatula and bake until the toothpick inserted into the center comes out clean, about 30 minutes. Let cool in the pan about 15 minutes. Cut into 8 squares to serve warm.

Sour Cream–Pecan Coffee Cake

There's nothing like coffee cake warm from the oven, especially if it takes only
15 minutes to prepare. A few time-saving tips—make the batter in the same
food processor that you've just made the topping in; use brown sugar in
both the topping and the cake (no need to get out the white sugar, too,
and brown sugar gives the cake a rich flavor and color); put the topping
in the freezer while you make the batter to ensure that it will stay
crumbly (and not completely melt) during baking.

MAKES ONE 8-INCH SQUARE CAKE; 8 SERVINGS

EQUIPMENT

Measuring cups and measuring spoons

8-inch square baking pan

Nonstick cooking spray

Food processor fitted with metal blade

Butter knife

Cutting board

Small bowl

Rubber spatula

Toothpick

INGREDIENTS

1/2 cup pecans

10 tablespoons (1 1/4 sticks) unsalted butter, softened

1 1/2 cups light brown sugar

1 1/2 cups plus 2 tablespoons all-purpose flour

1 teaspoon ground cinnamon

1/2 teaspoon baking powder

1/2 teaspoon baking soda

1/2 teaspoon salt

1/2 cup sour cream

2 large eggs

1. Preheat the oven to 350 degrees. Spray the
baking pan with cooking spray.

2. Place the pecans in the work bowl of the
food processor and pulse two or three times to
coarsely chop. Cut 2 tablespoons of the butter
into 1/4-inch pieces and add to the work bowl
along with 1/2 cup of the brown sugar,
2 tablespoons of the flour, and the cinnamon.
Pulse once or twice to combine; do not
overprocess. The mixture should be crumbly,

and not hold together. Transfer the topping to the small bowl and place in the freezer while preparing the batter.

3. Combine the remaining 1 cup brown sugar, 1½ cups flour, the baking powder, baking soda, and salt in the work bowl of the food processor (it is not necessary to wash the bowl) and pulse once or twice to combine. Cut the remaining 8 tablespoons butter into 8 or so pieces and add to the food processor along with the sour cream.

Process until moistened. Add the eggs and process, scraping down the bowl two or three times as necessary, until the batter is smooth.

4. Scrape the batter into the prepared pan, smooth the top with the spatula, and sprinkle with the pecan mixture. Bake until the toothpick inserted into the center comes out clean, 35 to 40 minutes. Let cool in the pan about 15 minutes, cut into squares, and serve warm.

By adding ingredients or making substitutions in the recipe for
Sour Cream–Pecan Coffee Cake, you can make a different coffee cake
for every day of the week.

◆

Hazelnut–Chocolate Chip Coffee Cake. Substitute skinned and chopped hazelnuts for the pecans. Omit the cinnamon. Add ½ cup miniature chocolate chips to the batter before scraping it into the pan.

Raspberry-Almond Coffee Cake. Substitute chopped almonds for the pecans. Add ½ teaspoon pure almond extract to the batter. Omit the cinnamon. Scatter ¾ cup raspberries over the batter before sprinkling with the crumbs.

Blueberry-Walnut Coffee Cake. Substitute chopped walnuts for the pecans. Scatter ¾ cup fresh blueberries over the batter in the pan before sprinkling with the crumbs.

Prune-Ginger Coffee Cake. Add ½ teaspoon ground ginger to the crumbs. Add ½ cup finely chopped pitted prunes to the batter (make sure the pieces are very small, so they don't sink to the bottom of the pan).

Oatmeal-Currant Coffee Cake. Substitute chopped walnuts for the pecans. Add ¼ cup rolled oats to the crumbs. Add ½ cup finely chopped currants to the batter.

Coconut Crunch Coffee Cake. Omit the cinnamon. Add ½ cup sweetened flaked coconut and 1 teaspoon pure vanilla extract to the batter.

Olive Oil and Orange Cake

This is a moist, not too sweet cake. Olive oil gives it an intriguing (and not specifically olive-y) flavor. Save very pungent oils for salad dressings and choose a relatively mild (but not "light," since these have no flavor at all) olive oil for baking.

MAKES ONE 8-INCH SQUARE CAKE; 8 SERVINGS

EQUIPMENT

Measuring cups and measuring spoons
Citrus zester
8-inch square baking pan
Nonstick cooking spray
Large bowl
Electric mixer fitted with paddle attachment
Rubber spatula
Toothpick
2 wire racks
Small fine-mesh strainer

INGREDIENTS

*1½ cups cake flour or all-purpose flour, plus more
    for dusting the pan*
¾ cup sugar
1 teaspoon baking soda
½ teaspoon salt
1 cup orange juice
⅓ cup extra-virgin olive oil
1 teaspoon grated orange zest
Confectioners' sugar for dusting

1. Preheat the oven to 350 degrees. Spray the baking pan with cooking spray, dust with flour, and tap out any excess.

2. Combine the flour, sugar, baking soda, and salt in the bowl. Add the orange juice, olive oil, and orange zest and mix on medium-low speed with the mixer until well combined.

3. Scrape the batter into the prepared pan with the spatula. Bake until the toothpick inserted into the center comes out clean and the sides of the cake begin to pull away from the pan, 30 to 35 minutes. Let cool in the pan on a wire rack about 10 minutes, invert the pan onto another rack, and then reinvert on the first rack to let cool completely. To serve, sift the confectioners' sugar over the cake with the strainer and slice into squares.

Simple Pine Nut Cake

This simple but sophisticated dessert is a cross between a cake and a cookie— thin wedges of cake topped with toasted pine nuts. Serve with glasses of dessert wine, as a change from the usual biscotti.

ONE 8-INCH CAKE; 6 SERVINGS

EQUIPMENT

Measuring spoons and measuring cups

Butter knife

Butter warmer or small saucepan

8-inch round cake pan

Nonstick cooking spray

Large bowl

Electric mixer fitted with paddle attachment

Wooden spoon

Rubber spatula

2 wire racks

Small fine-mesh strainer

INGREDIENTS

6 tablespoons (¾ stick) unsalted butter

3 large egg yolks

6 tablespoons sugar

1 teaspoon pure almond extract

⅔ cup all-purpose flour, plus more for dusting the pan

½ cup pine nuts

Confectioners' sugar for dusting

1. Preheat the oven to 350 degrees. Melt the butter in the butter warmer or saucepan and remove from the heat. Spray the cake pan with cooking spray, dust with flour, and tap out any excess.

2. Combine the egg yolks, sugar, and almond extract in the bowl and beat on high speed with the mixer until thick and pale, about 5 minutes. Stir in the flour until just combined.

3. Scrape the batter into the prepared pan and smooth the top with the spatula. Sprinkle the pine nuts evenly over the top of the cake. Bake until golden, 22 to 25 minutes. Let cool in the pan on a wire rack about 10 minutes, invert the pan onto another rack, and then reinvert on the first rack to let cool completely. Sift confectioners' sugar over the cake with the strainer before serving.

Pecan-Bourbon Cake

This Southern-inspired cake has a sandy texture and a pronounced aroma of bourbon. Thin slices of this rich, sweet cake should more than satisfy.

MAKES ONE 9-INCH CAKE; 8 TO 10 SERVINGS

EQUIPMENT

Measuring cups and measuring spoons
9-inch round cake pan
Nonstick cooking spray
Food processor fitted with metal blade
Small bowl
Rubber spatula
2 wire racks

INGREDIENTS

1⅓ cups cake flour or all-purpose flour, plus extra
*   for dusting the pan*
1 cup pecans
½ cup (1 stick) unsalted butter, softened
1 cup firmly packed light brown sugar
1 large egg
2 tablespoons bourbon
¼ teaspoon pure vanilla extract
4 teaspoons baking powder
¼ teaspoon salt

1. Preheat oven to 350 degrees. Prepare the pan with cooking spray and flour; tap out excess.

2. Grind the pecans in the food processor until fine. Don't overprocess, or the nuts will release their oil and you'll have nut butter rather than a dry powder. Transfer to the small bowl.

3. Combine the butter and brown sugar in the food processor (you don't have to wash it out) and process until smooth, scraping down the sides of the bowl once or twice. With the motor running, add the egg, bourbon, and vanilla through the feed tube and process until smooth, scraping down the sides of the bowl. Add the 1⅓ cups flour, the baking powder, salt, and pecans and pulse to incorporate.

4. Scrape the batter into the prepared pan, smooth the top with the spatula, and bake until a toothpick inserted into the center comes out clean, 40 to 45 minutes. Let cool in the pan on a wire rack about 10 minutes, invert the pan onto another rack, and then reinvert on the first rack to cool completely.

Apricot-Almond Cake

The food processor saves precious minutes in this recipe, mixing the batter as well as chopping the almonds and apricots. Chop the apricots and almonds finely, or they may sink to the bottom of the pan. I like this not-too-sweet cake for breakfast or an afternoon snack.

MAKES ONE 9-INCH CAKE; 6 TO 8 SERVINGS

EQUIPMENT

Measuring cups and measuring spoons

Butter knife

9-inch round cake pan

Nonstick cooking spray

Food processor fitted with metal blade

2 small bowls

Rubber spatula

2 wire racks

INGREDIENTS

⅔ cup all-purpose flour, plus extra for dusting the pan

1⅔ cups blanched almonds

1 cup dried apricots

9 tablespoons unsalted butter, softened

1¼ cups sugar

5 large eggs

½ teaspoon baking powder

¼ teaspoon salt

2 tablespoons brandy

1. Preheat the oven to 350 degrees. Spray the cake pan with cooking spray, dust with flour, and tap out any excess.

2. Place ⅔ cup of the almonds in the work bowl of the food processor and grind until fine. Transfer to one of the bowls.

3. Place the remaining 1 cup almonds and the apricots in the work bowl of the food processor (you don't have to wash it out) and pulse several times to finely chop. Transfer to the other bowl.

4. Combine the butter and sugar in the work bowl of the food processor (you don't have to wash it out) and process until smooth, scraping down the sides of the bowl once or twice as necessary. With the motor running, add the eggs one at a time through the feed tube and

process until smooth, scraping down the sides of the bowl as necessary. Add the ground almonds and pulse once or twice to incorporate. Add the flour, baking powder, and salt and pulse once or twice to incorporate. Add the brandy and chopped almonds and apricots and pulse once or twice to incorporate. ◆

5. Scrape the batter into the prepared pan, smooth the top with the spatula, and bake until golden, 50 to 55 minutes. Let cool in the pan on a wire rack about 10 minutes, invert the pan onto another rack, and then reinvert on the first rack to let cool completely before serving.

Buttermilk-Cornmeal Cake with Berries and Cream

Cornmeal gives this food processor recipe a pleasant crunch. I love the combination of the lemony cake and blueberries, but other fruit—sliced peaches or apricots, for example—may be substituted.

MAKES ONE 9-INCH CAKE; 6 TO 8 SERVINGS

EQUIPMENT

Measuring cups and measuring spoons

Citrus zester

9-inch round cake pan

Nonstick cooking spray

Food processor fitted with metal blade

Rubber spatula

2 wire racks

Medium-size bowl

Electric mixer fitted with whisk attachment

INGREDIENTS

½ cup all-purpose flour, plus extra for dusting the pan

1 cup (2 sticks) unsalted butter, softened

1 cup plus 2 tablespoons sugar

4 large eggs

¼ cup buttermilk

2 teaspoons grated lemon zest

1 cup yellow cornmeal

1 teaspoon baking powder

½ teaspoon baking soda

¼ teaspoon salt

¾ cup heavy cream

1 pint fresh blueberries, washed and picked over for stems

1. Preheat the oven to 350 degrees. Spray the cake pan with cooking spray, dust with flour, and tap out the excess.

2. Combine the butter and 1 cup of the sugar in the work bowl of the food processor and process until smooth, scraping down the sides of the bowl once or twice as necessary. With the motor running, add the eggs one at a time

through the feed tube and process until smooth, scraping down the sides of the bowl as necessary. Add the buttermilk and lemon zest and pulse once or twice to incorporate. Add the cornmeal, flour, baking powder, baking soda, and salt and pulse once or twice to incorporate.

3. Scrape the batter into the prepared pan, smooth the top with the spatula, and bake until golden, 45 to 50 minutes. Let cool in the pan on a wire rack about 10 minutes, invert the pan onto another rack, and then reinvert on the first rack to let cool completely.

4. To serve: Place the heavy cream and the remaining 2 tablespoons sugar in the bowl and beat with the mixer on high speed until it holds stiff peaks. Cut the cake into wedges and set on dessert plates. Place a dollop of whipped cream next to each piece of cake and scatter blue berries around the plate.

Almond-Scented Cream Cake

This cake can simply be stirred together by hand, but an electric mixer cuts preparation time to under 10 minutes. Without any butter, it is drier than a conventional butter cake, and benefits from the moisture of macerated berries.

MAKES ONE 9-INCH CAKE; 6 TO 8 SERVINGS

EQUIPMENT

Measuring cups and measuring spoons

9-inch round cake pan

Nonstick cooking spray

Large bowl

Electric mixer fitted with paddle attachment

Wooden spoon

Rubber spatula

Toothpick

2 wire racks

Paring knife

Cutting board

Medium-size bowl

Spoon

INGREDIENTS

1½ cups cake flour or all-purpose flour, plus extra
    for dusting the pan

1 large egg

2 large egg yolks

¾ cup plus 1 tablespoon sugar

⅔ cup heavy cream

1 teaspoon pure vanilla extract

1 teaspoon pure almond extract

2 teaspoons baking powder

¼ teaspoon salt

1 pint fresh strawberries

1. Preheat the oven to 350 degrees. Spray the cake pan with cooking spray, dust with flour, and tap out any excess.

2. Combine the whole egg and yolks in the large bowl and beat with the mixer on medium speed until frothy, about 2 minutes. Add ¾ cup of the sugar, the heavy cream, and the vanilla and almond extracts. Beat until light, 2 to 3 minutes. Stir in the flour, baking powder, and salt.

3. Scrape the batter into the prepared pan, smooth the top with the spatula, and bake until the toothpick inserted into the center comes

out clean, about 30 minutes. Let cool in the pan on a wire rack about 10 minutes, invert the pan onto another rack, and then reinvert on the first rack to let cool completely.

4. Fifteen minutes before serving, trim the stems from the strawberries and thinly slice. Place in the medium-size bowl with the remaining 1 tablespoon sugar. Toss to combine and toss once or twice more to dissolve the sugar. Serve slices of the cake with the macerated berries.

Pumpkin-Spice Pound Cake

Pureed pumpkin makes this cake extra moist. The food processor makes preparation extra simple. I like this plain or toasted as an afternoon snack, or with a scoop of vanilla ice cream for dessert.

MAKES 8 TO 10 SERVINGS

EQUIPMENT

Measuring cups and measuring spoons

8 × 4-inch loaf pan

Nonstick cooking spray

Food processor fitted with metal blade

Cutting board

Butter knife

Rubber spatula

Toothpick

2 wire racks

INGREDIENTS

1½ cups all-purpose flour, plus extra for dusting the pan

1 cup sugar

1 teaspoon baking powder

½ teaspoon baking soda

¼ teaspoon salt

½ teaspoon ground cinnamon

¼ teaspoon ground nutmeg

½ cup (1 stick) unsalted butter

2 large eggs

One 15-ounce can pumpkin puree

1 teaspoon pure vanilla extract

1. Preheat the oven to 350 degrees. Spray the loaf pan with cooking spray, dust with flour, and tap out the excess.

2. Combine the 1½ cups flour, the sugar, baking powder, baking soda, salt, cinnamon, and nutmeg in the work bowl of the food processor and pulse once or twice. Cut the butter into 8 or so pieces and add to the bowl. Add one of the eggs. Process until the dry ingredients are moistened. With the machine running, add the remaining egg, the pumpkin puree, and vanilla through the feed tube and process until smooth, scraping down the sides of the bowl once or twice as necessary.

3. Scrape the batter into the prepared pan with the spatula and bake until the toothpick inserted into the center comes out clean, about 1 hour and 10 minutes. Let cool in the pan on a wire rack about 10 minutes, invert the pan onto another rack, and then reinvert on the first rack to cool completely.

Golden Honey Pound Cake

Substituting honey for most of the sugar gives this pound cake extra moistness and a flowery bouquet. Honey browns the cake quickly, so check on it frequently and tent it with aluminum foil if it gets too dark too soon. Lightly toast slices of this cake and serve with scoops of chocolate or vanilla ice cream when company comes over.

MAKES 8 TO 10 SERVINGS

EQUIPMENT

Measuring cups and measuring spoons

Citrus zester

8 × 4-inch loaf pan

Nonstick cooking spray

Food processor fitted with metal blade

Cutting board

Butter knife

Rubber spatula

Toothpick

Aluminum foil

2 wire racks

Small saucepan

Pastry brush

INGREDIENTS

3 cups all-purpose flour, plus extra for dusting the
    pan

¼ cup sugar

2 teaspoons baking powder

½ teaspoon salt

1 cup (2 sticks) unsalted butter

1¼ cups honey

3 large eggs

1 teaspoon grated lemon zest

2 tablespoons fresh lemon juice

1. Preheat the oven to 350 degrees. Spray the loaf pan with cooking spray, dust with flour, and tap out the excess.

2. Combine the 3 cups flour, the sugar, baking powder, and salt in the work bowl of the food processor and pulse once or twice. Cut the butter into 16 or so pieces and add to the bowl. Add 1 cup of the honey. Process until the dry ingredients are moistened. With the machine running, add the eggs, lemon zest, and

1 tablespoon of the lemon juice through the feed tube and process until smooth, scraping down the sides of the bowl once or twice as necessary.

3. Scrape the batter into the prepared pan with the spatula and bake until the toothpick inserted into the center comes out clean, about 1 hour and 10 minutes. Check on the cake after about 45 minutes. If you notice that it is very brown, tent a sheet of aluminum foil over the top for the remainder of the baking. Let cool in the pan on a wire rack about 10 minutes, invert the pan onto another rack, and then reinvert on the first rack to cool completely.

4. Heat the remaining ¼ cup honey and 1 tablespoon lemon juice in the saucepan until warm but not boiling. Brush the glaze on the top and sides of the warm cake and let the cake cool completely.

Lemon Cream Cupcakes

These lemony cupcakes contain a decadent surprise—a cream cheese filling that elevates them to true dessert heights.

MAKES 12 CUPCAKES

EQUIPMENT

Measuring cups and measuring spoons

Citrus zester

12-cup muffin tin

Nonstick cooking spray

Butter knife

Large bowl

Electric mixer fitted with paddle attachment

Rubber spatula

Small bowl

Fork

Spoon

Wire rack

Small fine-mesh strainer (optional)

INGREDIENTS

¾ cup (1½ sticks unsalted) butter, softened

1½ cups sugar

6 large eggs

¼ cup fresh lemon juice

2¼ cups cake flour or all-purpose flour

1½ teaspoons baking powder

½ teaspoon salt

1 tablespoon grated lemon zest

¾ cup cream cheese, softened

Confectioners' sugar for dusting (optional)

1. Preheat the oven to 350 degrees. Spray the muffin tin with cooking spray.

2. Combine the butter and 1¼ cups of the sugar in the large bowl and beat with the mixer on medium-high speed until fluffy. Add the eggs and 3 tablespoons of the lemon juice and beat until well combined, scraping down the bowl once or twice as necessary. Mix in the flour, baking powder, salt, and 2 teaspoons of the lemon zest until just combined.

3. In the small bowl, mash together the cream cheese, the remaining ¼ cup sugar, the remaining 1 tablespoon lemon juice, and the remaining 1 teaspoon lemon zest until combined.

4. Spoon about 3 tablespoons of the batter into each muffin cup. Place about 1 tablespoon of the cream cheese mixture on top of each portion of batter and cover the cheese with some of the remaining batter (the batter should reach three-quarters of the way to the top of each cup). Bake until golden, about 20 minutes. Let the cupcakes cool in the pan for 10 minutes before turning over onto the wire rack to cool completely. Use the strainer to sift the tops with confectioners' sugar before serving if desired.

Vanilla Bean Cupcakes

I like to bake traditional pound cake batter in
cupcake tins for the richest, tastiest cupcakes you'll ever have.
A vanilla bean gives the batter a beautiful aroma
and attractive dark flecks.

MAKES 12 CUPCAKES

EQUIPMENT

Measuring cups and measuring spoons
12 paper muffin cups
12-cup muffin tin
Cutting board
Food processor fitted with metal blade
Zippered-top plastic bag
Paring knife
Rubber spatula
Toothpick
Wire rack

INGREDIENTS

1½ cups cake flour or all-purpose flour
¾ cup sugar
¾ teaspoon baking powder
¼ teaspoon salt
13 tablespoons unsalted butter, softened

1 vanilla bean
3 large eggs

1. Preheat the oven to 350 degrees. Place the paper muffin cups into the muffin tin.

2. Combine the flour, sugar, baking powder, and salt in the work bowl of the food processor and pulse once or twice. Cut the butter into 13 or so pieces and add to the bowl. With the knife, split the vanilla bean in half lengthwise. Place one half in the plastic bag and reserve for another use. Scrape the seeds from the other half into the work bowl. Add one of the eggs and process until the dry ingredients are moistened. With the machine running, add the remaining 2 eggs one at a time through the feed tube and process until smooth, scraping down

the sides of the bowl once or twice as necessary.

3. Scrape the batter evenly into the prepared muffin tin and bake until the toothpick inserted into the center of one of the cupcakes comes out clean, 20 to 25 minutes. Let cool in the tin for about 5 minutes and then remove the cupcakes to the wire rack to cool completely.

Individual Molten Chocolate Cakes

This type of dessert has become obligatory on restaurant menus all over
the country in the past few years, but is really very simple to prepare at
home. It's just slightly underbaked cake batter (thus the puddinglike center)
served straight from the oven. This version doesn't require separating
the eggs and folding in the whites, which makes it a little more dense
(and quicker to prepare) than many restaurant varieties.

MAKES 4 CAKES

EQUIPMENT

Measuring cups and measuring spoons

Butter knife

Roasting pan

Double boiler or medium-size saucepan and
    medium-size stainless steel bowl

Chef's knife

Cutting board

2 wire whisks

Large bowl

Electric mixer fitted with paddle attachment

Medium-size bowl

Four 6-ounce ramekins or custard cups

Rubber spatula

Wire rack

INGREDIENTS

2 ounces bittersweet chocolate

1/4 cup (1/2 stick) unsalted butter

2 large eggs

1/2 teaspoon pure vanilla extract

1/2 cup sugar

1/4 cup all-purpose flour

1/4 cup unsweetened cocoa powder

1/4 teaspoon baking powder

1/8 teaspoon salt

1. Preheat the oven to 350 degrees. Place the
roasting pan in the oven and pour in 1/2 inch of
hot water.

2. Put 1 inch of water into the bottom of the
double boiler or saucepan and bring to a bare
simmer over medium-low heat. Finely chop the

chocolate. Combine the chocolate and butter in the top of the double boiler or in the steel bowl and place it over the simmering water, making sure that the water doesn't touch the bowl. Heat, whisking occasionally, until completely melted. Set aside to cool until barely warm.

3. While the chocolate and butter are melting, combine the eggs, vanilla, and sugar in the large bowl and beat with the mixer on medium-high speed until pale yellow, about 5 minutes.

4. Combine the flour, cocoa, baking powder, and salt in the medium-size bowl and whisk to combine and break up lumps.

5. Beat the melted chocolate into the egg mixture using the mixer on medium speed until well combined. Add the flour mixture and stir on low.

6. Scrape the batter into the ramekins with the spatula and carefully transfer them to the roasting pan. Bake until risen and cracked on top, 22 to 25 minutes. Let cool on the wire rack for 5 minutes and serve.

Oatmeal Shortcakes with Raspberries and Cream

This dessert pushes the 15-minute limit, since it has 3 components that must be prepared separately. Nonetheless, with a few time-saving tricks, it can be done. The shortcakes don't need to be rolled, just dropped in mounds, saving preparation time and giving the finished dessert a free-form, rustic look. Using raspberries means that you don't have to peel or slice the fruit—just mix with sugar a little ahead of time and then spoon onto the biscuits.

MAKES 6 SERVINGS

EQUIPMENT

Measuring cups and measuring spoons

Butter knife

Baking sheet

Parchment paper

Electric mixer fitted with paddle and whisk
  attachments

Spoon

Wire rack

Plastic wrap (optional)

2 medium-size bowls

Serrated knife

INGREDIENTS

2 cups all-purpose flour

½ cup rolled (old-fashioned) oats

1 tablespoon baking powder

½ teaspoon salt

3 tablespoons firmly packed light brown sugar

½ cup (1 stick) cold unsalted butter, cut into pieces

⅔ cup plus 1 tablespoon milk

¼ cup plus 2 teaspoons granulated sugar

1½ pints fresh raspberries

¾ cup heavy cream

1 tablespoon confectioners' sugar

1. Preheat the oven to 425 degrees. Line the baking sheet with parchment paper. Combine the flour, oats, baking powder, and salt in the

bowl of the electric mixer. Add the brown sugar and butter and mix on low speed with the mixer fitted with the paddle until the mixture resembles coarse meal. Add the milk and mix until the dough just comes together. Do not overmix, or your shortcakes will be tough.

2. Gently form the dough into 6 mounds and place at least 2 inches apart on the baking sheet. Sprinkle them with 2 teaspoons of the granulated sugar. Bake until golden, 25 to 30 minutes. Slide the parchment onto the wire rack and let cool. (Biscuits can be made 1 day in advance, covered with plastic wrap, and stored at room temperature.)

3. Ten minutes before serving, combine the raspberries and the remaining ¼ cup granulated sugar in one of the medium-size bowls. Toss to combine and toss once or twice more to dissolve the sugar.

4. Slice off the top third of each biscuit using the serrated knife. Place each biscuit bottom on a dessert plate. Beat the heavy cream with the confectioners' sugar in the other medium-size bowl with the mixer fitted with the wire whisk until the mixture holds stiff peaks. Spoon half the raspberries onto the bottom portion of the biscuits. Top with the whipped cream. Spoon the remaining raspberries and some juice over the cream. Cover with the biscuit tops. Serve immediately.

QUICKEST COMFORT FOOD

PUDDINGS, CUSTARDS, AND MOUSSES

CHOCOLATE AND ORANGE CANNOLI CREAM

MANGO-RUM FOOL

MOCHA MOUSSE

FRESH FIG MOUSSE

PEANUT BUTTER SEMIFREDDO

WHITE CHOCOLATE–MASCARPONE MOUSSE

COCONUT RICE PUDDING

BUTTERY BUTTERSCOTCH PUDDING

INDIAN PUDDING

WARM TAPIOCA WITH HONEYED ORANGES

TEA-INFUSED PANNA COTTA

ESPRESSO GELATINS

LEMON GELATIN WITH BERRIES

BLUEBERRY-MAPLE SEMIFREDDO

LEMON *POTS DE CRÈME*

GINGER-SPICED CUSTARDS

MINT CUSTARDS

CROISSANT PUDDING

BANANA-CARAMEL BREAD PUDDING

GRAPE CLAFOUTIS

WHEN ASKED TO RECALL FAVORITE CHILDHOOD SWEETS, most Americans will lovingly and longingly rhapsodize over butterscotch pudding, tapioca, and even Jell-O before they will consider the madeleine. So-called nursery foods were probably the first desserts most of us tasted and the ones we remember most fondly. How lucky we are! While Proust never could find a cookie comparable to the ones he snacked on as a kid, we can easily replicate and, in most cases, vastly improve on the comfort foods we grew up with.

Chief among child-pleasers is whipped cream, and this is where I begin. There is nothing like whipped cream for simultaneous richness and lightness. But plain, sweetened whipped cream is bland. It needs the addition of a strong flavoring ingredient to create excitement even as it comforts. The additions can range from pureed mango, lime juice, and rum in Mango-Rum Fool to bittersweet chocolate and instant espresso powder in Mocha Mousse to peanut butter and vanilla in Peanut Butter Semifreddo. Simply folding these extras into whipped cream creates incomparable desserts. Whipping cream is child's play, but if you are overenthusiastic and beat it too long, you *can* ruin it. Whip the cream just until it holds stiff peaks, but not even a few seconds

longer or it will be grainy and lumpy, not smooth the way you remember it.

A variety of rustic puddings provides similar nostalgic pleasures, with the added benefit (in my opinion) that many can be eaten warm. I've tried to update and improve some of these puddings while retaining the qualities that made them favorites in the first place. Coconut Rice Pudding is just as creamy and soothing as the diner variety, but the addition of coconut milk adds an extra layer of flavor that most adults will appreciate. Indian Pudding tastes the same as it always did, cornmeal enriched with egg and milk and distinctively sweetened with molasses. But by using instant polenta, my version requires a lot less stirring and precooking. If there is an essential piece of equipment for making any of these desserts, it is the wire whisk, which banishes lumps. Use a whisk if you want your desserts to have the perfect texture that will separate them from examples served at interstate truck stops.

Not all comfort foods are creamy or starchy. Desserts made with gelatin can be fat-free and refreshingly light. Lemon Gelatin with Berries recalls those Jell-O molds of the past, but with fresh berries and lemon juice instead of canned cherries and mini-marshmallows, it is utterly natural and wholesome-tasting. Espresso Gelatins are like shots of strong, sweetened coffee and make a wonderful substitute for after-dinner coffee on a hot summer night. You must warm granules of gelatin to dissolve them properly and make such sparkling desserts, but always heat gently, over barely simmering water or by stirring in warm, not boiling, liquid. When overcooked, gelatin will break down and fail to gel, leaving you with a beverage rather than a spoonable treat.

In my mind, custard desserts bridge the gap between childhood and adult pleasures. While I might make Warm Tapioca with Honeyed Oranges only for family and my most casual guests, I do not hesitate to serve Ginger-Spiced Custards or Mint Custards to a group that has just consumed my most expensive rack of lamb. What's good enough for patrons of Paris bistros, after all, is good enough to cap off my dinner parties. Of all the desserts in this chapter, egg custards are the most difficult to get right. They are easily prepared—just whisk together milk, cream, eggs, and sugar—but they should be strained before cooking to ensure smoothness. If overcooked or cooked too quickly, they will curdle, so they absolutely must be baked in a water bath. Remove them from the oven while they are still wobbly. They might look underdone, but they will finish cooking while they cool. If you wait until they look fully cooked, your custards will resemble scrambled eggs rather than silky cooked cream.

Puddings, custards, and mousses in other chapters:
Spiced Mexican Chocolate Pudding (page 18)
Blackberries with Champagne Sabayon (page 199)
Frozen Lemon Sabayon Terrine with Kiwis and
*   Raspberries (page 200)*

Chocolate and Orange Cannoli Cream

Sweetened ricotta cheese, eaten with a spoon rather than stuffed into a cannoli shell, is probably a 5-minute dessert, but no less satisfying for its effortlessness.

MAKES 4 SERVINGS

EQUIPMENT

Measuring cups and measuring spoons
Citrus zester
Medium-size bowl
Wooden spoon
Plastic wrap
4 dessert goblets

INGREDIENTS

2 cups whole-milk ricotta cheese
3 tablespoons confectioners' sugar
2 tablespoons heavy cream
1 teaspoon grated orange zest
1 teaspoon pure vanilla extract
¼ cup miniature chocolate chips
8 store-bought or homemade lace cookies
    (see 5 Minutes Extra) or four 2-inch-long pieces
    orange peel (optional)

1. Combine the ricotta, confectioners' sugar, heavy cream, orange zest, and vanilla in the bowl and stir until creamy. Stir in the chocolate chips. Cover with plastic wrap and refrigerate until ready to serve, up to 24 hours.

2. To serve, stir well and spoon the mixture into the dessert goblets. Serve with lace cookies or orange peel as a garnish, if desired.

Instead of filling cannoli shells with the cream, bake up a batch of Oatmeal Lace Cookies as a crisp counterpart. Lace cookies may take you 10 or 15 minutes, but considering how simple it is to make the cannoli cream, you might be able to spare the extra time. Preheat the oven to 325 degrees. Line a large baking sheet with parchment paper (parchment is essential here, since it will allow you to easily lift with your fingers the delicate cookies from the baking sheet without shattering them). Melt 6 tablespoons (¾ stick) unsalted butter in a medium-size saucepan. Remove from the heat and stir in ¾ cup rolled (old-fashioned) oats, 6 tablespoons granulated sugar, 1 tablespoon all-purpose flour, ¼ teaspoon salt, and ½ teaspoon pure vanilla extract. Stir in 1 large egg yolk. Drop the batter by table-spoonfuls onto the parchment, leaving at least 2½ inches between each cookie (they will spread). Bake until the edges are golden brown, 12 to 13 minutes. Slide the parchment onto a wire rack to cool. Using your fingers, lift the cookies from the parchment when completely cooled.

Mango-Rum Fool

A fool is about as simple a fruit dessert as you can make—just fold pureed fruit into whipped cream and serve. Here I use my favorite tropical fruit and enhance its citrusy sweetness with a little bit of lime juice and rum.

There are one or two tricks to peeling a mango and separating the flesh from the pit: Hold the mango in one hand, resting the stem end on the cutting board. With a sharp knife in the other hand, remove strips of skin, top to bottom, working around the fruit until all the skin is removed. Cut the flesh from the pit, again slicing from top to bottom, cutting all the way around the pit.

MAKES 4 SERVINGS

EQUIPMENT

Measuring cups and measuring spoons
Chef's knife
Cutting board
Food processor fitted with metal blade
Rubber spatula
Large bowl
Electric mixer fitted with whisk attachment
Plastic wrap
Spoon
4 dessert goblets

INGREDIENTS

2 ripe mangoes
1 tablespoon fresh lime juice
3 tablespoons confectioners' sugar
1 tablespoon dark rum
2/3 cup heavy cream

1. Peel the mangoes and cut the flesh from the pits. Combine the mango pieces, lime juice, 2 tablespoons of the confectioners' sugar, and the rum in the work bowl of the food processor and process until smooth, scraping down the sides of the bowl with the spatula once or twice as necessary.

2. Place the heavy cream and the remaining 1 tablespoon confectioners' sugar in the bowl and beat with the mixer on high speed until it holds stiff peaks. Gently fold in the mango mixture. Cover with plastic wrap and refrigerate for 1 hour or up to 4 hours. Spoon the fool into 4 dessert goblets and serve.

Mocha Mousse

Instant espresso powder gives eggless chocolate mousse a deep, rich flavor. This can be refrigerated for several hours before serving but, since it has no gelatin or other stabilizer, it will begin to separate if kept overnight.

MAKES 4 SERVINGS

EQUIPMENT

Measuring cups and measuring spoons
Double boiler or medium-size saucepan and
 medium-size stainless steel bowl
Chef's knife
Cutting board
Wire whisk
Large bowl
Electric mixer with whisk attachment
Plastic wrap
Rubber spatula
Spoon
4 dessert goblets

INGREDIENTS

6 ounces bittersweet chocolate
2 tablespoons sugar
¼ cup water
2 teaspoons instant espresso powder
1 cup heavy cream

1. Put 1 inch of water into the bottom of the double boiler or a saucepan and bring to a bare simmer over medium-low heat. Finely chop the chocolate. Combine the chocolate, sugar, water, and espresso powder in the top of the double boiler or in the steel bowl and set it over the simmering water, making sure that the water doesn't touch the bowl. Heat, whisking occasionally, until the chocolate is completely melted and the sugar and espresso granules are dissolved. Set aside to cool until barely warm to the touch.

2. Place the heavy cream in the bowl and beat with the mixer on high speed until it holds stiff peaks. Gently fold in the chocolate mixture with the spatula. Cover with plastic wrap and refrigerate up to 6 hours before spooning into dessert goblets to serve.

◆

If you'd like, garnish each portion of mousse with

a dollop of Kahlúa-flavored whipped cream

(1/3 cup heavy cream whipped to stiff peaks

with 1 tablespoon confectioners' sugar and

1 tablespoon Kahlúa) and/or a chocolate-covered

espresso bean.

Fresh Fig Mousse

Here is an adaptation of a favorite recipe from Colman Andrews' book *Catalan Cuisine*. Figs, walnuts, and anisette are a classic Spanish combination. The best figs are not necessarily the most beautiful—look for fruit that is fragrant and soft (it might even ooze a little bit) around the stem.

MAKES 4 SERVINGS

EQUIPMENT

Measuring cups and measuring spoons
Chef's knife
Cutting board
Medium-size bowl
2 spoons
Fork
Large bowl
Electric mixer fitted with whisk attachment
Rubber spatula
Plastic wrap
4 dessert goblets

INGREDIENTS

½ cup walnuts
3 pounds fresh figs
1 teaspoon Sambuca or other anisette liqueur
2 cups heavy cream
2 tablespoons confectioners' sugar

4 walnut halves for garnish (optional)

1. Finely chop the walnuts and place in the medium-size bowl. Slice each fig in half lengthwise and scrape the pulp into the bowl with a spoon. Discard the skins. Add the Sambuca and gently mash with the fork to combine.

2. Place the heavy cream and confectioners' sugar in the large bowl and beat with the mixer on high speed until the mixture holds stiff peaks. Gently fold in the fig mixture with the spatula. Cover with plastic wrap and refrigerate until ready to serve, up to 6 hours. To serve, spoon the mousse into 4 dessert goblets and garnish each with a walnut half if desired.

Peanut Butter Semifreddo

It's amazing how a few staple ingredients can so quickly become a
special dessert. I like to garnish cups of the semifreddo with shards of chocolate bar.
You can dip them into the semifreddo for a peanut butter cup effect.
For more elaborate treatments, see 5 Minutes Extra.

MAKES 4 SERVINGS

EQUIPMENT

Measuring cups and measuring spoons
Large bowl
Electric mixer fitted with whisk attachment
Small bowl
Rubber spatula
Plastic wrap
Ice cream scoop
4 dessert goblets

INGREDIENTS

1 cup heavy cream
7 tablespoons confectioners' sugar
1 teaspoon pure vanilla extract
½ cup smooth peanut butter
4 ounces bittersweet chocolate, broken into
    shards

1. Combine the heavy cream, confectioners'
sugar, and vanilla in the large bowl and beat
with the mixer on high speed until the mixture
holds stiff peaks.

2. Place the peanut butter in the small bowl and
stir in one quarter of the whipped cream.
Gently fold the lightened peanut butter mixture
back into the remaining whipped cream using
the spatula. Cover with plastic wrap and freeze
for at least 1 hour and up to 24 hours.

3. To serve, scoop some of the semifreddo into
each dessert goblet and garnish with the
chocolate shards. Serve immediately.

5 MINUTES EXTRA

*To take this to the next level, serve over
Bittersweet Chocolate Waffles (page 28). To gild
the lily, pour Warm Chocolate Sauce (page 133)
over the semifreddo-topped waffles.*

White Chocolate–Mascarpone Mousse

On its own, white chocolate can be cloyingly sweet. Combined with heavy cream and tangy mascarpone (available in Italian groceries, cheese shops, and many supermarkets), it becomes an incomparably rich and satisfying mousse. Buy best-quality white chocolate—Lindt and Baker's are two good brands widely available. Cheap white chocolate doesn't have the cocoa butter content that gives the dessert its great flavor.

MAKES 4 SERVINGS

EQUIPMENT

Measuring cups and measuring spoons
Double boiler or medium-size saucepan and
    medium-size stainless steel bowl
Chef's knife
Cutting board
Wire whisk
Large bowl
Electric mixer fitted with whisk attachment
Rubber spatula
Plastic wrap
Spoon
4 dessert goblets

INGREDIENTS

6 ounces white chocolate
½ cup plus 3 tablespoons heavy cream
2 tablespoons water
2 tablespoons light corn syrup
4 ounces mascarpone cheese (about ½ cup)
16 to 20 fresh raspberries or blackberries

1. Put 1 inch of water into the bottom of the double boiler or saucepan and bring to a bare simmer over medium-low heat. Finely chop the chocolate. Combine the chocolate, 3 tablespoons of the heavy cream, the water, and corn syrup in the top of the double boiler or the steel bowl and set it over the simmering

water, making sure that the water doesn't touch the bowl. Heat, whisking occasionally, until the chocolate is completely melted. Set aside to cool until barely warm to the touch. Whisk in the mascarpone.

2. Place the remaining ½ cup heavy cream in the bowl and beat with the mixer on high speed until the mixture holds stiff peaks. Gently fold in the chocolate mixture using the spatula. Cover with plastic wrap and refrigerate at least 4 hours and up to 24 hours. To serve, spoon the mousse into 4 dessert goblets and garnish with the berries.

Coconut Rice Pudding

Creamy rice pudding is an old, familiar favorite. When made with coconut milk instead of cream, it becomes a little exotic. Although you have to stir the pudding a few times during its 45 minutes of cooking, actual preparation time is in the 5-minute range.

MAKES 6 SERVINGS

EQUIPMENT

Measuring cups and measuring spoons
Paring knife
Zippered-top plastic bag
Medium-size saucepan
Wooden spoon
Glass bowl or 6 custard cups or dessert goblets
Plastic wrap

INGREDIENTS

1 vanilla bean
1 cup long-grain rice
One 14-ounce can unsweetened coconut milk
3 cups whole milk
¾ cup sugar
2 tablespoons chopped crystallized ginger (optional)

1. With the paring knife, split the vanilla bean in half lengthwise. Place one half in the plastic bag and reserve for another use. Scrape the seeds from the other half into the saucepan and add the scraped half of the bean. Add the rice, coconut milk, milk, and sugar and bring to a boil. Reduce the heat to medium-low and cook at a bare simmer, uncovered, stirring occasionally with the wooden spoon, until the rice is tender and almost all the liquid has been absorbed, 45 to 50 minutes.

2. While the rice is cooking, finely chop the crystallized ginger if desired.

3. Discard the vanilla bean. Spoon the pudding into the glass bowl or divide the puddings among custard cups or dessert goblets. Serve warm, or cover the surface of the pudding with plastic wrap, chill, and serve cold. Sprinkle each

serving with 1 teaspoon chopped crystallized ginger before serving if desired. Coconut Rice Pudding can be refrigerated, covered with plastic wrap, up to 2 days.

Warm Chocolate Sauce dresses up Coconut Rice Pudding. To make the sauce, finely chop 5 ounces bittersweet chocolate and place in a heatproof bowl. Bring ¾ cup heavy cream to a boil in a small saucepan. Pour over the chocolate, cover the bowl with plastic wrap, and let stand for 5 minutes. Whisk until smooth. Mound some of the chilled pudding in each of 6 dessert goblets and drizzle the sauce over each pudding. Garnish with a piece of crystallized ginger, if desired, and serve.

Buttery Butterscotch Pudding

Dark brown sugar is essential here—it gives the pudding its butterscotch flavor. This is rich, so portions are small. If you are in a hurry for pudding, let this cool 5 minutes and eat it warm. If you can wait, place some plastic wrap directly on each pudding (so you don't get that dread "pudding skin") and refrigerate before serving.

MAKES 4 SERVINGS

EQUIPMENT

Measuring cups and measuring spoons
Butter knife
Medium-size saucepan
Wire whisk
Small bowl
Spoon
4 ramekins or dessert goblets
Plastic wrap

INGREDIENTS

3 tablespoons unsalted butter
½ cup firmly packed dark brown sugar
Pinch of salt
3 tablespoons cornstarch
1 cup milk
1 cup heavy cream

1. Combine the butter, brown sugar, and salt in the saucepan. Cook over low heat, whisking, until the butter is melted and the sugar is dissolved.

2. Combine the cornstarch and ½ cup of the milk in the bowl and whisk to dissolve. Set aside.

3. Add the remaining ½ cup of themilk to the saucepan and whisk until the milk and brown sugar mixture are combined. Add the heavy cream and the cornstarch mixture to the saucepan, stir to combine, and turn the heat to medium-high. Continue to cook over medium-high heat, whisking, until the mixture thickens, 3 to 4 minutes. Remove from the heat and spoon into the ramekins or dessert goblets. Cover the surface of each pudding with a piece of plastic wrap to prevent a skin from forming. Refrigerate up to 24 hours and serve cold.

Indian Pudding

Using instant polenta rather than cornmeal saves time and muscle. With cornmeal, you must whisk the pudding constantly for 15 to 20 minutes before baking. With instant polenta, a minute or two will do. I serve this New England classic with vanilla ice cream, but it is also good with whipped cream, sour cream, or crème fraîche.

MAKES 6 SERVINGS

EQUIPMENT

Measuring cups and measuring spoons
8-inch square baking dish
Nonstick cooking spray
Medium-size saucepan
Wire whisk
Wooden spoon
Fork
Small bowl

INGREDIENTS

2¾ cups whole milk
½ cup instant polenta
2 tablespoons dark molasses
3 tablespoons sugar
½ teaspoon ground cinnamon
¼ teaspoon salt
1 large egg yolk
1 pint vanilla ice cream, softened a bit (optional)

1. Preheat the oven to 300 degrees. Spray the baking dish with cooking spray. Place 2½ cups of the milk in the saucepan and bring to a boil. Whisk in the polenta and simmer, whisking frequently, until the mixture begins to thicken, 1 to 2 minutes. Remove from the heat and stir in the molasses, sugar, cinnamon, and salt.

2. Lightly beat the yolk in the bowl. Dribble a little of the hot cornmeal mixture into the bowl as you whisk. Return the egg mixture to the saucepan and whisk to combine.

3. Pour the pudding into the baking dish and pour the remaining ¼ cup milk over the pudding. Do not stir it in. Bake until set, about 2 hours. Let cool slightly and serve warm with ice cream if desired.

Warm Tapioca with Honeyed Oranges

I like tapioca when it has started to set up but is still warm—not only is it classically comforting this way, but you only have to wait a few minutes from the time you remove it from the stovetop before digging in. Orange slices warmed in a bit of honey are a cheerful garnish. Be sure to buy navel oranges (no seeds) and remove as much of the tough white pith as possible.

MAKES 4 SERVINGS

EQUIPMENT

Measuring cups and measuring spoons

Medium-size saucepan

Wire whisk

Paring knife

Wooden spoon

Large bowl filled with ice water

Medium-size skillet

Spoon for serving

4 dessert goblets

INGREDIENTS

3 tablespoons quick-cooking tapioca

5 tablespoons sugar

¼ teaspoon salt

2 large eggs

2 cups milk

2 medium-size navel oranges

½ teaspoon pure vanilla extract

2 tablespoons honey

4 sprigs fresh mint (optional)

1. Place the tapioca, sugar, salt, eggs, and milk in the saucepan and whisk to combine. Let stand for 5 minutes without stirring to swell the tapioca.

2. While the tapioca is standing, peel and section the oranges. Remove the white pith from each section with a paring knife.

3. Cook the tapioca mixture over medium-high heat, stirring, until it comes to a boil. Simmer for 1 minute and remove from the heat. Stir in the vanilla. Place the saucepan in the bowl of ice water and let stand, stirring once or twice, until thickened but still warm, 3 to 4 minutes.

4. While the tapioca is cooling, combine the honey and orange sections in the skillet and cook over medium heat until just warm.

5. To serve: Spoon the warm tapioca into the goblets. Spoon a few honeyed orange slices over each portion. Garnish with a mint sprig if desired.

Tea-Infused Panna Cotta

Intrigued by a recipe for a traditional tea custard in Jean Anderson's *The Food of Portugal*, I wondered how I could simplify it. Instead of baking a cream, egg, and tea mixture, I decided to make a tea-flavored panna cotta—a no-bake gelatin-and-cream dessert that's a lot less tricky. If you enjoy coffee- or espresso-flavored desserts, give this a try. Garnish with a dollop of whipped cream, or serve with any cookies or biscuits that you would serve with after-dinner tea.

MAKES 6 SERVINGS

EQUIPMENT

Measuring cups and measuring spoons
Small saucepan
Wire whisk
Double boiler or medium-size saucepan and medium-size stainless steel bowl
Six 8-ounce ramekins
Plastic wrap
Small bowl
Paring knife
6 small dessert plates

INGREDIENTS

3 cups half-and-half
6 tablespoons sugar
2 bags strong tea such as Earl Gray or Darjeeling
1 packet (2 teaspoons) unflavored gelatin

1. Heat 1½ cups of the half-and-half and the sugar in the saucepan, whisking to dissolve the sugar. Bring the mixture just to a boil and remove from the heat. Add the tea bags and let steep for 5 minutes.

2. Meanwhile, bring 1 inch of water to a bare simmer in the bottom of the double boiler or saucepan. Pour the remaining 1½ cups half-and-half into the top of the double boiler or the steel bowl. Sprinkle the gelatin over the half-and-half to dissolve it.

3. Remove the tea bags from the cream-and-sugar mixture. Set the gelatin-sprinkled half-and-half over the simmering water and add the tea mixture. Whisk until the gelatin is

completely dissolved, 2 to 3 minutes. Pour the mixture into the ramekins. Cover with plastic wrap and refrigerate until set, at least 6 hours or overnight.

4. To unmold the panna cottas, fill a small bowl with very hot tap water. Run the paring knife around each panna cotta to separate it from the sides of the ramekin and then dip the bottom half of the ramekin in the water for 30 seconds. Place a dessert plate on top of the mold, invert, tap the bottom of the mold, and lift the mold off the plate. Serve immediately.

Espresso Gelatins

Instead of coffee and dessert, combine the two in this simple, do-ahead sweet.
A serving of this dessert is equivalent to a double espresso, so use decaf
if you're concerned about sleep.

MAKES 4 SERVINGS

EQUIPMENT

Measuring cups and measuring spoons
Small stainless steel bowl
Wire whisk
4 small dessert goblets
Plastic wrap
Medium-size bowl
Electric mixer fitted with whisk attachment
Spoon

INGREDIENTS

2 tablespoons water
1 packet (2 teaspoons) unflavored gelatin
*2 cups hot brewed espresso or very strong brewed
  coffee*
5 tablespoons sugar
⅓ cup heavy cream

1. Place the water in the steel bowl and sprinkle the gelatin over the water. Let stand to dissolve, 1 to 2 minutes.

2. Add the hot espresso and 4 tablespoons of the sugar and whisk until the gelatin and sugar are completely dissolved, 2 to 3 minutes. Pour into the goblets. Cover with plastic wrap and refrigerate until set, at least 6 hours or overnight.

3. Place the heavy cream and the remaining 1 tablespoon sugar in the medium-size bowl and beat with the mixer on high speed until the mixture holds stiff peaks. Top each goblet of gelatin with a dollop of whipped cream and serve immediately.

Lemon Gelatin with Berries

This is an incredibly simple and light summer dessert, as pretty to look at as it is refreshing to the palate. Other berries (blackberries, blueberries, sliced strawberries) may be substituted if you like.

MAKES 4 SERVINGS

EQUIPMENT

Measuring cups and measuring spoons

Citrus zester

2 small bowls

Medium-size saucepan

Wire whisk

Medium-size bowl

Spoon

Plastic wrap

4 dessert goblets or sundae glasses

INGREDIENTS

2 envelopes (4 teaspoons total) unflavored gelatin

2½ cups cold water

1 cup plus 1 tablespoon sugar

1 cup fresh lemon juice (juice from 5 or 6 large lemons)

½ teaspoon grated lemon zest

1 pint fresh raspberries

1. In one of the small bowls, sprinkle the gelatin over ½ cup of the cold water and let soften for 2 minutes. Combine the remaining 2 cups cold water, 1 cup of the sugar, the lemon juice, and zest in the saucepan and bring to a boil. Remove from the heat and whisk in the gelatin mixture. Whisk for 1 minute to dissolve any lumps. Pour into the medium-size bowl, cover the bowl with the plastic, and refrigerate until firm, at least 6 hours and up to 1 day.

2. Combine the berries and the remaining 1 tablespoon sugar in the other small bowl and let stand, stirring once or twice, until the sugar dissolves, about 10 minutes. Spoon a few raspberries into the bottom of each goblet or sundae glass. Spoon half the lemon gelatin into the goblets. Top with half the remaining raspberries. Divide the remaining lemon gelatin among the goblets or glasses and top with the remaining raspberries. Serve immediately.

Blueberry-Maple Semifreddo

A generous amount of maple syrup sweetens this simple frozen dessert, perfect for casual summer entertaining. Grade B syrup, which is darker and stronger (and cheaper), gives you the most flavor for your money.

MAKES 6 SERVINGS

EQUIPMENT

Measuring cups and measuring spoons

1½-quart bowl

Plastic wrap

Double boiler or medium-size saucepan and medium-size stainless steel bowl

Wire whisk

Large bowl

Electric mixer fitted with whisk attachment

Rubber spatula

Large serving plate

Chef's knife

INGREDIENTS

1 cup pure maple syrup

1 packet (2 teaspoons) unflavored gelatin

2 cups heavy cream

½ teaspoon pure maple extract

1 pint fresh blueberries, picked over for stems

1. Line the bowl with plastic wrap, making sure that the wrap lies flat and that there is at least 1 inch overhanging the top of the bowl on all sides.

2. Bring 1 inch of water to a bare simmer in the bottom of the double boiler or in the saucepan. Pour the maple syrup into the top of the double boiler or the steel bowl. Sprinkle the gelatin over the syrup. Set the maple syrup over the simmering water. Whisk until the gelatin is completely dissolved, 2 to 3 minutes.

3. Place the heavy cream and maple extract in the large bowl and beat with the mixer on high speed until the mixture holds stiff peaks. Gently but quickly fold in the maple syrup mixture using the spatula. Fold in the berries. Scrape the semifreddo into the prepared bowl, smooth the

top with the spatula, and cover with plastic wrap. Freeze at least 6 hours and up to 24 hours.

4. To unmold, gently tug the plastic wrap that lines the bowl to loosen the semifreddo. Place the serving plate over the bowl and turn it over. Gently tap to release the semifreddo. Peel the plastic wrap from the semifreddo and cut into wedges with the chef's knife. Serve immediately.

Lemon *Pots de Crème*

This bistro classic is also one of the easiest baked custards you can put together. Lemon zest, rather than juice, gives the custard just the right amount of lemon flavor; it is refreshingly, not mouth-puckeringly, tart.

MAKES 4 SERVINGS

EQUIPMENT

Measuring cups and measuring spoons

Citrus zester

Roasting pan

Small saucepan

Wire whisk

Medium-size bowl

Small fine-mesh strainer

Large glass measuring cup

Four 6-ounce custard cups or ramekins

Aluminum foil

Wire rack

INGREDIENTS

1 cup whole milk

1 cup heavy cream

1 large egg

3 large egg yolks

⅓ cup granulated sugar

2 teaspoons grated lemon zest

1 tablespoon confectioners' sugar for dusting (optional)

1. Preheat the oven to 350 degrees. Place the roasting pan in the oven and pour ½ inch of hot water into it.

2. Combine the milk and heavy cream in the saucepan and bring almost to a boil. Remove from the heat.

3. Whisk the whole egg, egg yolks, and granulated sugar together in the bowl. Slowly whisk in the hot cream, beginning with a dribble and graduating to a thin stream.

4. Place the strainer on top of the measuring cup and strain the custard mixture into it. Stir in the lemon zest.

5. Pour the custard evenly into the custard cups or ramekins, open the oven, and carefully place them into the pan with the water (the water

should reach about halfway up the sides of the cups). Cover loosely with a sheet of aluminum foil and bake until the sides of the custards are set but the centers still wobble when gently shaken, 28 to 30 minutes. Do not overcook the custards or they will be curdled, not silky smooth.

6. Carefully remove the water-filled pan from the oven, remove the custard cups or ramekins from the pan, and let cool on the wire rack for 20 minutes at room temperature before chilling until serving, at least 4 hours or overnight. With the washed strainer, sift some confectioners' sugar over each *pot de crème* immediately before serving if desired.

Egg-based desserts like the custards and bread puddings in this chapter, as well as Easiest, Best Chocolate Mousse Cake (page 84) and Individual Molten Chocolate Cakes (page 113), must be baked in a water bath. A water bath provides a shield between delicate egg mixtures and the heat of the oven, allowing for slow cooking that results in silky smooth desserts. Baked without a water bath, these desserts would cook too quickly and curdle, resembling scrambled eggs in texture.

While the concept is simple, the process of actually getting your desserts into and out of a water bath is fraught with pitfalls. Here are a few tips to help you along:

Choose a roasting pan that's about the same depth or just a little bit deeper than your dessert dish or pan. If the sides of the roasting pan are much deeper, it will slow down or even prevent complete cooking as the higher sides will impede heat circulation.

For Easiest, Best Chocolate Mousse Cake, or for any recipe that requires a springform pan to be placed in a water bath, remember to place the pan on a piece of heavy-duty aluminum foil and mold the foil to the sides, but not over the top, of the pan to keep water from seeping in.

Many people suggest pouring boiling water from a measuring cup into the roasting pan after you've transferred the ramekins, baking dish, or springform pan. This is fine if you are confident that you will not splash the water onto the dessert or on yourself in the process. For even moderately klutzy people like myself, it's easier to fill the roasting pan with ½ inch of hot tap water before you even start cooking, place it in the oven, turn the oven on, and proceed with the recipe. When the dessert is ready to go into the oven, carefully place it in the preheated water. A half inch of water should be just enough so that it comes halfway up the sides of any dishes used in the recipes in this book.

It is easier to remove the roasting pan from the oven with the dessert still in it than to try to take the dessert out of the pan while the pan is still in the oven. I bake bread puddings in ceramic dishes with little ears or handles. Wearing oven mitts, it is simple enough to remove these dishes from the water bath for cooling on a wire rack. Springform pans require more careful handling. I find oven mitts too cumbersome for grasping the sides of the pan, and always wind up dipping them in the hot water. Square pot holders are less bulky. Ramekins are the most difficult to get out of hot water. I use heavy-duty spring-loaded tongs or a long-handled, wide metal spatula; with oven mitts or pot holders I have a hard time picking up the ramekins without sticking part of the mitt into the surface of the custard.

Ginger-Spiced Custards

A small amount of ground ginger gives plain custard some spice.

MAKES 4 SERVINGS

EQUIPMENT

Measuring cups and measuring spoons

Roasting pan

Small saucepan

Wire whisk

Medium-size bowl

Small fine-mesh strainer

Large glass measuring cup

Four 6-ounce custard cups or ramekins

Aluminum foil

Wire rack

INGREDIENTS

1 cup whole milk

1 cup heavy cream

1 teaspoon ground ginger

1 large egg

3 large egg yolks

⅓ cup sugar

1. Preheat the oven to 350 degrees. Place the roasting pan in the oven and pour ½ inch of hot water into it.

2. Combine the milk, heavy cream, and ginger in the saucepan and bring it almost to a boil. Remove from the heat.

3. Whisk the whole egg, egg yolks, and sugar together in the bowl. Slowly whisk in the hot cream, beginning with a dribble and graduating to a thin stream.

4. Place the strainer on top of the measuring cup and strain the hot custard mixture into it.

5. Pour the custard into the custard cups or ramekins, open the oven, and carefully place them into the pan with the water (the water should reach about halfway up the sides of the cups). Cover loosely with a sheet of aluminum foil and bake until the sides of the custards are set but the centers still wobble when gently

shaken, 28 to 30 minutes. Do not overcook the custards or they will be curdled, not silky smooth.

6. Carefully remove the pan from the oven, remove the custard cups or ramekins from the pan, and let cool on the wire rack for 20 minutes at room temperature before chilling until serving, at least 4 hours or overnight.

Mint Custards

I tried to make mint custards with fresh mint leaves several times, but no matter how long I steeped the leaves in the hot cream and milk, I couldn't get enough flavor out of the leaves to make it worthwhile. Mint extract, on the other hand, lends fantastic flavor in seconds. I do like the dark flecks and potent aroma of a vanilla bean here, but if you'd like, you can substitute ½ teaspoon vanilla extract and stir it in with the mint extract. Sometimes a garnish of fresh mint leaves seems fussy, but in this case it makes perfect sense as a signal of what you will taste when you dip your spoon in this creamy but fresh-tasting custard.

MAKES 4 SERVINGS

EQUIPMENT

Measuring cups and measuring spoons
Roasting pan
Small saucepan
Paring knife
Zippered-top plastic bag
Wire whisk
Medium-size bowl
Small fine-mesh strainer
Large glass measuring cup
Four 6-ounce custard cups or ramekins
Aluminum foil
Wire rack

INGREDIENTS

1 cup whole milk
1 cup heavy cream
1 vanilla bean
¼ teaspoon pure mint extract
1 large egg
3 large egg yolks
⅓ cup sugar
4 sprigs fresh mint for garnish

1. Preheat the oven to 350 degrees. Place the roasting pan in the oven and pour ½ inch of hot water into it.

2. Combine the milk and heavy cream in the saucepan. With the paring knife, split the vanilla bean in half lengthwise. Place one half in the plastic bag and reserve for another use. Scrape the seeds from the other half into the pan and add the scraped bean half to the pan. Bring almost to a boil. Remove from the heat and stir in the mint extract.

3. Whisk the whole egg, egg yolks, and sugar together in the bowl. Slowly whisk in the hot cream, beginning with a dribble and graduating to a thin stream.

4. Place the strainer on top of the measuring cup and strain the hot custard mixture into it.

5. Pour the custard evenly into the custard cups or ramekins, open the oven, and carefully place them into the pan with the water (the water should reach about halfway up the sides of the cups). Cover loosely with a sheet of aluminum foil and bake until the sides of the custards are set but the centers still wobble when gently shaken, 28 to 30 minutes. Do not overcook the custards or they will be curdled, not silky smooth.

6. Carefully remove the pan from the oven, remove the custard cups from the pan, and let cool for 20 minutes on the wire rack at room temperature before chilling until serving, at least 4 hours or overnight. Garnish with mint sprigs before serving.

Croissant Pudding

An effortless way to elevate basic bread pudding is to substitute croissants for day-old bread. To keep down the cost of this luxurious-tasting dessert, check the better bakeries in your area—many sell day-old croissants at half-price.

MAKES 6 SERVINGS

EQUIPMENT

Measuring cups

Large roasting pan

7 x 11-inch glass or porcelain baking dish

Cutting board

Bread knife

Paring knife

Zippered-top plastic bag

Electric mixer fitted with paddle attachment

Wooden spoon

Wire rack

INGREDIENTS

¾ cup golden raisins

3 to 4 large day-old croissants (about 12 ounces total)

3 cups whole milk

3 large eggs

2 large egg yolks

¾ cup sugar

1 vanilla bean

1. Preheat the oven to 350 degrees. Place the roasting pan in the oven and pour ½ inch of hot water into it.

2. Scatter the raisins across the bottom of the glass baking dish. Cut the croissants into ½-inch-thick slices and place on top of the raisins in the dish.

3. Combine the milk, whole eggs, egg yolks, and sugar in the bowl of an electric mixer fitted with a paddle. With the paring knife, split the vanilla bean in half lengthwise. Place one half in the plastic bag and reserve for another use. Scrape the seeds from the other half into the bowl. Discard the scraped bean half. Beat on medium-low speed with the mixer until well blended and a little frothy, 1 to 2 minutes.

4. Pour the egg mixture over the croissants and press the bread with the back of the spoon to

make sure that everything is submerged. Let stand a minute or two, pressing with the spoon once or twice, to allow the bread to absorb the egg mixture. Carefully place the dish in the pan of hot water and bake until golden and just set, about 50 minutes.

5. Carefully remove the roasting pan from the oven, then remove the baking dish from the pan and let cool on the wire rack. Serve slightly warm or let cool completely, refrigerate covered with plastic wrap up to 24 hours, and serve chilled.

Banana-Caramel Bread Pudding

A ribbon of caramelized bananas running through
this bread pudding is a happy surprise.

MAKES 6 SERVINGS

EQUIPMENT

Measuring cups and measuring spoons

Large roasting pan

Cutting board

Chef's knife

Medium-size saucepan

Spoon

7 x 11-inch glass or porcelain baking dish

Large bowl

Electric mixer fitted with paddle attachment

Wire rack

INGREDIENTS

¾ cup walnuts

3 ripe bananas

¼ cup (½ stick) unsalted butter

⅔ cup firmly packed dark brown sugar

½ cup heavy cream

1 teaspoon pure vanilla extract

1 day-old loaf French or Italian bread (about 12 ounces)

3 cups whole milk

3 large eggs

2 large egg yolks

½ cup granulated sugar

1. Preheat the oven to 350 degrees. Place the roasting pan in the oven and pour ½ inch of hot water into it.

2. Coarsely chop the walnuts. Peel and slice the bananas into ½-inch-thick rounds.

3. Heat the butter in the saucepan over medium-high heat. Add the brown sugar and stir until dissolved, about 1 minute. Add the heavy cream and cook until slightly thickened, about 1 minute. Stir in the walnuts, sliced bananas, and vanilla. Set aside.

4. Cut the bread into ½-inch-thick slices and place half of the slices in the baking dish. Spoon the banana mixture evenly over the bread. Top with the remaining bread slices.

5. Combine the milk, whole eggs, egg yolks, and granulated sugar in the bowl. Beat on medium-low speed with the mixer until well blended and a little frothy, 1 to 2 minutes.

6. Pour the egg mixture over the bread and press the bread with the back of the spoon to make sure that everything is submerged. Let stand a minute or two, pressing with the spoon once or twice to allow the bread to absorb the egg mixture. Carefully place the dish in the pan of hot water and bake until golden and just set, about 50 minutes.

7. Carefully remove the roasting pan from the oven, then remove the baking dish from the pan and let cool on the wire rack. Serve slightly warm or let cool completely, refrigerate covered with plastic wrap up to 24 hours, and serve chilled.

Grape Clafoutis

This fruit-and-custard dessert couldn't be easier. Butter is
melted in the baking dish while you assemble the rest of the ingredients.
Cherries are traditional but seedless grapes are quicker, since there's no need
to pit them. A glass or ceramic baking dish produces the best browning,
but a cake pan may be used in a pinch.

MAKES 6 TO 8 SERVINGS

EQUIPMENT
Measuring cups and measuring spoons
10-inch round glass or ceramic baking dish
Food processor fitted with metal blade
Rubber spatula
Wire rack

INGREDIENTS
¾ pound red seedless grapes
¼ cup (½ stick) unsalted butter
6 large eggs
½ cup plus 2 tablespoons sugar
1 cup whole milk
1 teaspoon pure vanilla extract
⅔ cup all-purpose flour
Pinch of salt

1. Preheat the oven to 400 degrees. Stem the grapes. Place the butter in the baking dish and place the dish in the oven.

2. While the butter melts, combine the eggs, ½ cup of sugar, the milk, and vanilla extract in the food processor by pulsing two or three times. Add the flour and salt and pulse to blend.

3. Remove the baking dish from the oven and tilt to distribute the butter evenly over the bottom. Pour the batter into the pan (the butter might sizzle a little). Stir once or twice with the spatula to incorporate the butter. Don't worry if the butter pools in spots. Scatter the grapes

across the top. Sprinkle with the remaining
2 tablespoons sugar. Bake until the batter is
firm and golden, 30 to 35 minutes. Remove
from the oven and let cool on the rack for 10 to
15 minutes. Serve warm, in wedges.

QUICK BITES

COOKIES

AND CANDY

MAPLE WALNUT MERINGUES

CHOCOLATE MERINGUE KISSES

FIG AND ALMOND MERINGUES

CLASSIC SCOTTISH SHORTBREAD

BROWN SUGAR SHORTBREAD

MOCHA SHORTBREAD

LEMON-CREAM CHEESE SHORTBREAD

CRANBERRY BUTTER COOKIES

ANISE-FLAVORED BUTTER COOKIES

MEXICAN WEDDING CAKES

HOMEMADE VANILLA WAFERS

GIANT COCONUT-CASHEW COOKIES

CHEWY GINGER-MOLASSES COOKIES

DELUXE FOUR-LAYER BARS

NUT BUTTER BLONDIES

SWEET AND SPICY PECAN BRITTLE

HONEY AND ALMOND BRITTLE

HOMEMADE GRANOLA BARS

WHITE CHOCOLATE-MINT TRUFFLES

MACADAMIA NUT FUDGE

CHANCES ARE GOOD THAT IF YOU ARE READING A BOOK called *Instant Gratification* you've had your lapses of self-control with regard to dessert. And if you are like me, you are especially apt to lose it around cookies and candy. My feeling about this weakness is, if it's not curable, then at least let it be utterly pleasurable. Instead of hating myself afterward for devouring a box of dry-as-dust, store-bought cookies or a bag of low-quality miniature candy bars, I indulge myself with a batch of Brown Sugar Shortbread or Macadamia Nut Fudge. I probably have thousands of cookie and candy recipes in my cookbook library, but the ones I come back to over and over are like these— quick enough that they're almost effortless, good enough to spark cravings again soon after I've finished off the batch.

To keep these recipes especially quick, I've stuck to simple mixtures of just a few ingredients. There probably won't be any complaints when these ingredients include combinations like dried figs and almonds (Fig and Almond Meringues) or cashews and coconut (Giant Coconut-Cashew Cookies). None of the cookies need to be rolled and cut. None are iced or filled. I've also kept the quantities small. Not only does it take less time to make a dozen cookies than it does to make a hundred, it makes binging on the products of your (very little) labor less dangerous to your waistline.

There are several categories of cookies and candy that lend themselves to 15-minute preparation. A relatively new favorite of mine is meringues, simple confections that contain no butter and flour, just egg whites and sugar, whipped until fluffy and baked until crisp. Plain meringues are a little too plain for my taste but, with the addition of chocolate, dried fruit, and/or nuts, meringues are cookies to be reckoned with.

Next on the list is shortbread, also relatively

simple because it contains no eggs—just flour, sugar, and butter. I like to bake my shortbread in a tart pan and cut the baked dough into wedges with fluted edges. Just patting the dough into place is quicker than rolling it out. An added benefit is that the finished cookies look great. This way, for example, Mocha Shortbread is pretty enough for company when served sticking out of dessert goblets mounded with coffee ice cream. Lemon–Cream Cheese Shortbread is a terrific accompaniment for mixed berries and fruit sorbet.

There is a reason why butter cookies prevail in most kitchens. Nothing telegraphs "home baking" more than the combination of eggs, sugar, flour, and generous amounts of butter. An electric mixer stirs together the dough in no time. If the dough is simply dropped onto baking sheets, preparation is minimal. But I don't love butter cookies just because they are easy. Butter cookie dough is the perfect medium for a variety of delicious and surprising tastes. Dried cranberries make plain cookies sparkle. Anise seeds are a simple way to transform cookie dough into an exotic taste sensation. Even Homemade Vanilla Wafers are like nothing you've ever had when made with cake flour and an abundance of vanilla.

Bar cookies have always been touted as quicker, since, instead of dropping the dough onto cookie sheets, you simply dump it into a baking pan. Figuring that you've already got a favorite brownie recipe, I've included just a couple of ideas for making special bar cookies. One temptation is just to throw everything you can think of into the mixer, so I try to stop and think before I bake. By limiting myself to four favorite ingredients, I think I bake a better, as well as quicker, "layer bar." Likewise, I like a minimalist granola bar, with just one kind of dried fruit and one kind of nut. This way, I can really enjoy the combination of golden raisins and walnuts, or dried cherries and almonds, rather than wondering what exactly I'm eating. And as always, high-quality ingredients ensure a stellar end product. A luxury item like hazelnut butter transforms boring blondies into truly special squares.

Rounding out the chapter are a few candy recipes. I've always found candy-making scary. There's the thermometer, there are those mysterious terms like "soft-ball" and "hard-crack." No need to worry here. Sweet and Spicy Pecan Brittle requires no special equipment or vocabulary. With only a saucepan, a few minutes, and a watchful eye, you can transform nuts, sugar, and spices into wonderfully shiny caramel candy. Making

White Chocolate Mint Truffles is as simple as melting white chocolate in hot cream and stirring in mint extract. Since the coating is cocoa powder rather than melted dark chocolate, there's no need to worry about "tempering," or anything else, except whether or not you'll have enough candy to go around. ◆

Other instantly gratifying cookie and candy recipes:

Tiny Coconut Macaroons (page 23)

Oatmeal Lace Cookies (page 123)

Parmesan Shortbreads with Red Wine Strawberries (page 202)

Maple Walnut Meringues

By virtue of their short ingredients lists, meringues are among the quickest cookies to put together. Any finely chopped nut can be added to beaten egg whites. I like to add a little maple extract to give these simple treats an extra layer of flavor. Be careful when handling these—they have a wonderfully delicate texture, but shatter easily.

MAKES ABOUT 28 COOKIES

EQUIPMENT

Measuring cups and measuring spoons
2 baking sheets
Parchment paper
Food processor fitted with metal blade
Large bowl
Electric mixer with whisk attachment
Rubber spatula
2 wire racks

INGREDIENTS

¾ cup walnuts
1 cup sugar
3 large egg whites
2 teaspoons pure maple extract

1. Position 2 oven racks in the top third and bottom third of the oven. Preheat the oven to 275 degrees. Line the baking sheets with parchment paper. Combine the walnuts and ¼ cup of the sugar in the work bowl of the food processor. Grind until fine.

2. Place the egg whites in the bowl and beat on medium speed with the electric mixer until frothy, about 30 seconds. Turn the speed to high and pour the remaining ¾ cup sugar into the bowl in a slow, steady stream. Continue to beat until the egg whites are stiff and shiny. Fold in the nut mixture and maple extract with the spatula, being careful not to deflate the meringue.

3. Spoon heaping tablespoonfuls of the batter onto the baking sheets, 1½ inches apart from one another. Bake until cooked through, about 35 minutes. Let cool on the baking sheets for 5 minutes before transferring to the wire racks.

Chocolate Meringue Kisses

These little cookies resemble big Hershey's Kisses, and will please anyone who loves chocolate. Miniature chocolate chips are best here, since they are light enough to stay suspended in the meringue mixture; large ones sink to the bottom.

MAKES ABOUT 28 COOKIES

EQUIPMENT

Measuring cups and measuring spoons
2 baking sheets
Parchment paper
Large bowl
Electric mixer with whisk attachment
Small fine-mesh strainer
Rubber spatula
2 wire racks

INGREDIENTS

3 large egg whites
1 cup sugar
2 tablespoons unsweetened cocoa powder
6 ounces miniature chocolate chips

1. Position 2 oven racks in the top third and bottom third of the oven. Preheat the oven to 275 degrees. Line the baking sheets with parchment paper. Place the egg whites in the bowl and beat with the electric mixer on medium speed until frothy, about 30 seconds. Turn the speed to high and pour the sugar into the bowl in a slow, steady stream. Continue to beat until the egg whites are stiff and shiny.

2. Hold the strainer over the bowl with the egg whites and sift the cocoa powder into the bowl. Pour the chocolate chips into the bowl. Fold together the ingredients with the spatula, being careful not to deflate the meringue.

3. Spoon heaping tablespoonfuls of the batter onto the baking sheets, 1½ inches apart from one another. Bake until firm on the outside but still soft on the inside, about 30 minutes. Let cool on the baking sheets for 5 minutes before transferring to the wire rack.

Fig and Almond Meringues

One of my favorite dessert combinations—figs and almonds—works wonderfully as an addition to beaten egg whites.

MAKES ABOUT 28 COOKIES

EQUIPMENT

Measuring cups and measuring spoons
2 baking sheets
Parchment paper
Large bowl
Electric mixer with whisk attachment
Food processor fitted with metal blade
Cutting board
Chef's knife
Rubber spatula
2 wire racks

INGREDIENTS

3 large egg whites
1 cup sugar
½ cup whole almonds
½ cup dried figs
1 teaspoon pure vanilla extract

1. Position 2 oven racks in the top third and bottom third of the oven. Preheat the oven to 275 degrees. Line the baking sheets with parchment paper. Place the egg whites in the bowl and beat with the electric mixer on medium speed until frothy, about 30 seconds. Turn the speed to high and pour ¾ cup of the sugar into the bowl in a slow, steady stream. Continue to beat until the egg whites are stiff and shiny.

2. While the egg whites are whipping, combine the almonds and the remaining ¼ cup sugar in the work bowl of the food processor. Grind until fine. Stem and finely chop the figs.

3. Fold the vanilla, ground almonds, and figs into the meringue with the spatula, being careful not to deflate the meringue.

4. Spoon heaping tablespoonfuls of the batter onto the baking sheets, 1½ inches apart from one another. Bake until cooked through, about 35 minutes. Let cool on the baking sheets for 5 minutes before transferring to the wire racks.

Classic Scottish Shortbread

Classic shortbread, with only 3 ingredients, is super-speedy to put together. If you'd like, you'll have the extra time to roll the dough ¼ inch thick and cut with a favorite cookie cutter. Do take the time to refrigerate the dough before baking. If you don't, your cookies will melt before they bake. You can even freeze the rolled dough and place it directly in the oven from the freezer. If you have a shortbread mold, go ahead and use it, but a 9-inch tart pan works just as well.

MAKES 12 SHORTBREAD WEDGES OR 16 2-INCH SQUARES

EQUIPMENT

Measuring cups

Paring knife

Large bowl

Electric mixer fitted with paddle attachment

Rolling pin

9-inch fluted tart pan with removable bottom or 8-inch square baking pan

Ruler or other straight edge

Fork

Plastic wrap

Wire rack

INGREDIENTS

1 cup (2 sticks) unsalted butter, chilled

½ cup sugar

2 cups all-purpose flour, plus more for rolling

1. Cut the butter into 12 pieces. Beat the butter and sugar together in the bowl with the electric mixer on medium-high speed until fluffy, 3 to 4 minutes.

2. Add the flour to the bowl and beat on the lowest speed until the dough just comes together. Do not overmix.

3. Lightly flour your work surface and turn the dough onto the surface. Roll the dough into a rough 9-inch circle or 8-inch square. Trim with the paring knife and fit into the pan. With the ruler as guide, score with the paring knife into 12 wedges or squares and prick all over with the fork. Cover with plastic wrap and refrigerate for 1 hour or up to 24 hours, or

freeze for up to 2 weeks and place in the oven directly to bake, removing the plastic wrap.

4. Preheat the oven to 250 degrees. Bake until the shortbread is firm but not colored, about 45 minutes. Let cool completely on the wire rack and cut the shortbread into wedges or squares with the paring knife.

Brown Sugar Shortbread

These shortbread cookies are especially quick to prepare since they contain only a few ingredients and they don't have to be rolled, but simply patted into a pan. I like to use a fluted tart pan, and then cut the cookies into pretty wedges, but a square baking pan works just as well. Brown sugar gives the cookies a rich, butterscotch flavor. Serve alone with coffee or tea, or with dishes of super-premium vanilla or coffee ice cream.

MAKES 12 SHORTBREAD WEDGES OR 16 2-INCH SQUARES

EQUIPMENT

Measuring cups and measuring spoons
Large bowl
Electric mixer fitted with paddle attachment
9-inch fluted tart pan with removable bottom or
    8-inch square baking pan
Nonstick cooking spray
Small bowl
Wire rack
Paring knife

INGREDIENTS

1 cup (2 sticks) unsalted butter, softened
1 cup firmly packed dark brown sugar
1 tablespoon granulated sugar
1 teaspoon ground cinnamon
2 cups all-purpose flour
¼ teaspoon salt

1. Preheat the oven to 325 degrees.

2. Beat the butter and brown sugar together in the large bowl with the electric mixer on medium-high speed until fluffy, 3 to 4 minutes. Coat the tart pan or baking pan with cooking spray. Combine the granulated sugar and cinnamon in the small bowl.

3. Add the flour and salt to the bowl with the butter and brown sugar and beat on the lowest speed until the dough just comes together. Do not overmix.

4. Turn the dough into the prepared pan and press the dough to the edges with your fingertips. Sprinkle with the cinnamon-sugar.

Bake until the shortbread is firm at the edges but still soft in the center, about 50 minutes. Let cool completely on the wire rack, then cut the shortbread into wedges or squares with the paring knife.

Mocha Shortbread

These thin cookies are crisp, not chewy, making them ideal for dunking in a tall glass of milk. They have an intense coffee flavor thanks to some instant espresso powder, one of my favorite ingredients for instant gratification. As always, I recommend using a high-quality unsweetened cocoa like Pernigotti for the richest chocolate taste.

MAKES 12 SHORTBREAD WEDGES OR 16 2-INCH SQUARES

EQUIPMENT

Measuring cups and measuring spoons
Electric mixer fitted with paddle attachment
9-inch fluted tart pan with removable bottom or
 8-inch square baking pan
Nonstick cooking spray
Small fine-mesh strainer
Paring knife
Wire rack

INGREDIENTS

½ cup (1 stick) unsalted butter, softened
½ cup sugar
¾ cup all-purpose flour
1 tablespoon instant espresso powder
⅛ teaspoon salt
½ cup unsweetened cocoa powder, plus more for
 sprinkling

1. Preheat the oven to 350 degrees.

2. Beat the butter and sugar in the bowl with the electric mixer on medium-high speed until fluffy, 3 to 4 minutes. Coat the tart pan or baking pan with cooking spray.

3. Add the flour, espresso powder, and salt to the bowl. Sift the ½ cup cocoa powder into the bowl through the strainer. Beat on the lowest speed until the dough just comes together. Do not overmix.

4. Turn the dough into the prepared pan. Lightly flour your hands and press the dough to the edges with your fingertips. Bake until the shortbread is firm at the edges but still soft in the center, about 25 minutes. Let cool for

10 minutes, then cut the shortbread into wedges or squares with the paring knife. Let cool completely on the wire rack before removing from the pan. Sprinkle with additional cocoa powder, using the strainer, before serving. ◆

Lemon–Cream Cheese Shortbread

These shortbreads are soft and cakey, perfect with a cup of tea. Cream cheese and a little lemon zest give them a rich, tangy taste. Orange zest may be substituted for the lemon for a slightly different citrus flavor.

MAKES 12 SHORTBREAD WEDGES OR 16 2-INCH SQUARES

EQUIPMENT

Measuring cups and measuring spoons
Citrus zester
Large bowl
Electric mixer fitted with paddle attachment
9-inch fluted tart pan with removable bottom or
    8-inch baking pan
Nonstick cooking spray
Wire rack
Paring knife

INGREDIENTS

½ cup (1 stick) unsalted butter, softened
One 8-ounce package cream cheese, softened
1¼ cups confectioners' sugar
1 teaspoon pure vanilla extract
1 teaspoon grated lemon zest
2 cups all-purpose flour

1. Preheat the oven to 375 degrees.

2. In the bowl, beat the butter, cream cheese, and confectioners' sugar together with the mixer on medium-high speed until fluffy, 3 to 4 minutes. Coat the tart pan or baking pan with cooking spray.

3. Add the vanilla and zest to the bowl and mix to combine. Add the flour to the bowl and beat on the lowest speed until the dough just comes together. Do not overmix.

4. Turn the dough into the prepared pan and press to the edges with your fingertips. Bake until the shortbread is golden and has begun to pull away from the side of the pan, about 25 minutes. Let cool completely on the wire rack, then cut the shortbread into wedges or squares with the paring knife.

Cranberry Butter Cookies

The addition of dried cranberries to simple butter cookie dough makes a delicate but interestingly tart cookie. Other dried fruits—try blueberries or cherries—may be substituted.

MAKES ABOUT 12 COOKIES

EQUIPMENT

Measuring cups and measuring spoons

Butter knife

Large baking sheet

Nonstick cooking spray

Large bowl

Electric mixer fitted with paddle attachment

Rubber spatula

Wire rack

INGREDIENTS

¼ cup (½ stick) unsalted butter, softened

¼ cup sugar

1 large egg

1 teaspoon pure vanilla extract

½ cup all-purpose flour

Pinch of salt

½ cup dried cranberries

1. Preheat the oven to 350 degrees. Spray the baking sheet with cooking spray.

2. In the bowl, beat together the butter and sugar with the mixer on medium-high speed until well combined. Add the egg and vanilla and beat, scraping down the sides of the bowl once or twice, until well combined. Mix in the flour and salt with the spatula until just combined. Mix in the cranberries.

3. Drop rounded teaspoonfuls of the batter on the prepared baking sheet, leaving 2 inches between each cookie. The cookies will spread quite a lot during baking. Bake until the edges have browned and the tops of the cookies are set, 10 to 12 minutes. Remove the baking sheet from the oven and let the cookies firm up on the cookie sheet for 5 minutes. Transfer the cookies to the wire rack to cool completely.

Anise-Flavored Butter Cookies

In Mexico, these traditional Christmas cookies are made with lard.
As always in baking, I prefer butter.

MAKES ABOUT 12 LARGE COOKIES

EQUIPMENT

Measuring cups and measuring spoons

Butter knife

Large baking sheet

Nonstick cooking spray

Large bowl

Electric mixer fitted with paddle attachment

Rubber spatula

Small bowl

Wire rack

INGREDIENTS

¼ cup (½ stick) unsalted butter, softened

½ cup sugar

1 teaspoon anise seeds

1 large egg

1½ cups all-purpose flour

½ teaspoon baking powder

¼ teaspoon salt

1. Preheat the oven to 350 degrees. Spray the baking sheet with cooking spray.

2. In the large bowl, beat together the butter, 6 tablespoons of the sugar, and the anise seeds with the mixer on medium-high speed until well combined. Add the egg and beat, scraping down the sides of the bowl once or twice with the spatula, until well combined. Mix in the flour, baking powder, and salt with the spatula until just combined.

3. Place the remaining 2 tablespoons sugar in the small bowl. With floured hands, roll rounded tablespoonfuls of the dough into balls. Dip the tops of the balls in the sugar and place, sugared side up, on the prepared baking sheet, leaving 2 inches between each cookie. Flatten each ball slightly with the palm of your hand. Bake until the bottoms of the cookies are golden, 20 to 22 minutes. Transfer the cookies to the wire rack to cool.

Mexican Wedding Cakes

As their name implies, these meltingly delicious cookies are special enough for the most momentous occasions. Even so, they couldn't be quicker to put together. Other nuts—try skinned hazelnuts or unsalted pistachios—may be substituted.

MAKES ABOUT 16 COOKIES

EQUIPMENT

Measuring cups and measuring spoons
Butter knife
Large bowl
Electric mixer fitted with paddle attachment
Food processor fitted with metal blade
Rubber spatula
Large baking sheet
Wire rack
Shallow bowl

INGREDIENTS

10 tablespoons (1¼ sticks) unsalted butter, softened
¼ cup granulated sugar
½ teaspoon salt
1 cup pecan halves
1 teaspoon water
1 teaspoon pure vanilla extract
1½ cups all-purpose flour
3 tablespoons confectioners' sugar

1. Preheat the oven to 325 degrees.

2. In the large bowl, beat together the butter, granulated sugar, and salt with the mixer on medium-high speed until well combined.

3. Finely chop the pecans in the work bowl of the food processor.

4. Beat the water and vanilla into the butter mixture. Mix in the flour with the spatula until just combined. Mix in the pecans.

5. Roll rounded tablespoonfuls of the dough into balls. Place on the baking sheet, leaving 1½ inches between each cookie. Bake until cooked through but not dry, about 20 minutes. Transfer the cookies to a wire rack to cool. Place the confectioners' sugar in the shallow bowl. When the cookies are completely cooled, roll in the confectioners' sugar to coat.

Homemade Vanilla Wafers

I wanted to include this recipe in the first chapter, but it took my oven too long
to get to 400 degrees for me to make, bake, and serve the cookies in 15 minutes;
start to finish, I make, bake, and serve these in about 18 minutes. The cookies are
soft, buttery, and perfumed with vanilla. They are simple, but very memorable—
free-form madeleines. If you don't have cake flour, you may substitute
regular all-purpose. The cookies won't be quite as tender, but they
will be wonderful nonetheless.

MAKES ABOUT 20 COOKIES

EQUIPMENT
Measuring cups and measuring spoons
Butter knife
Large baking sheet
Nonstick cooking spray
Large bowl
Electric mixer fitted with paddle attachment
Rubber spatula
Wire rack

INGREDIENTS
¼ cup (½ stick) unsalted butter, softened
6 tablespoons sugar
2 large egg yolks
1 tablespoon pure vanilla extract
6 tablespoons all-purpose flour

¼ cup cake flour
½ teaspoon baking powder
Pinch of salt

1. Preheat the oven to 400 degrees. Spray the
baking sheet with cooking spray.

2. In the bowl, beat together the butter and sugar
with the mixer on medium-high speed until well
combined. With the mixer running, add the
yolks one at a time, stopping in between each
addition to scrape down the sides of the bowl
with the rubber spatula. Beat in the vanilla.

3. Stir in the flours, baking powder, and salt
with the rubber spatula until just combined.

4. Drop rounded teaspoonfuls of the batter on the prepared baking sheet, leaving 1½ inches between each cookie. Bake until the edges have browned and the tops of the cookies are set, 7 to 8 minutes. Remove the baking sheet from the oven and let the cookies firm up on the sheet for 2 minutes. Transfer the cookies to the wire rack with the metal spatula to cool completely.

◆

Giant Coconut-Cashew Cookies

You can make these chewy-crispy cookies smaller, but they're more fun when they're big. They spread quite a lot during baking, and will break if you try to remove them from the baking sheet while very hot, so let them stand 5 to 10 minutes before transferring to a wire rack.

MAKES ABOUT 8 LARGE COOKIES

EQUIPMENT

Measuring cups and measuring spoons

Small saucepan

Wooden spoon

Large bowl

2 large baking sheets

Nonstick cooking spray

Cutting board

Chef's knife

Metal spatula

Wire rack

INGREDIENTS

¼ cup (½ stick) unsalted butter

1 cup firmly packed dark brown sugar

½ cup cashews

1 large egg

1 teaspoon pure vanilla extract

½ cup all-purpose flour

1 teaspoon baking powder

½ teaspoon salt

¾ cup sweetened flaked coconut

1. Preheat the oven to 350 degrees. Heat the butter and brown sugar together in the saucepan over medium heat, stirring occasionally, until the butter is melted and combined with the sugar. Scrape into the bowl and let cool slightly.

2. While the butter and sugar are cooling, spray the baking sheets with cooking spray. Coarsely chop the cashews.

3. Stir the egg and vanilla into the butter mixture. Stir in the flour, baking powder, and salt until just combined. Stir in the cashews and coconut. Place the bowl in the freezer for 3 to 4 minutes to allow the batter to firm up.

4. Drop large (about 3 tablespoons) spoonfuls of the batter on the prepared baking sheets, leaving 3 inches between each cookie. Bake until the cookies are just set, 10 to 12 minutes.

Remove the baking sheets from the oven and let the cookies firm up, 5 to 10 minutes. With a metal spatula, transfer the cookies to the wire rack to let cool completely.

Chewy Ginger-Molasses Cookies

This has been a favorite cookie of mine since I bought my very first
cookie sheet. I am always amazed at the fantastic flavor I get from
just a few pantry staples and spice-rack standbys.

MAKES ABOUT 18 COOKIES

EQUIPMENT

Measuring cups and measuring spoons

Butter knife

Butter warmer or small saucepan

Large baking sheet

Nonstick cooking spray

Medium-size bowl

Wooden spoon

Large bowl

Wire rack

Metal spatula

INGREDIENTS

6 tablespoons (¾ stick) unsalted butter

1 cup all-purpose flour

1 teaspoon ground ginger

½ teaspoon ground cinnamon

¼ teaspoon salt

¼ teaspoon baking soda

½ cup sugar

2 tablespoons dark molasses

1 large egg yolk

1. Preheat the oven to 350 degrees. Melt the
butter in the butter warmer or saucepan over
medium heat. Spray the baking sheet with
cooking spray.

2. Combine the flour, ginger, cinnamon, salt,
and baking soda in the medium-size bowl and
stir to combine.

3. Pour the melted butter into the large bowl
and stir in the sugar, molasses, and egg yolk.
Stir in the flour mixture until just combined.

4. Drop tablespoonfuls of the batter onto
the prepared baking sheet, leaving 3 inches
between each cookie. Bake until set, but
still soft in the center, 8 to 10 minutes. Let

cool for 5 minutes on the baking sheet
before removing to the wire rack with a
metal spatula.

5 MINUTES EXTRA

I love the combination of spicy ginger and

bittersweet chocolate. If you do, too, and you have

an extra 5 minutes, try this: When your cookies

have cooled, melt 2 ounces bittersweet chocolate

in the top of a double boiler over simmering

water. Dip half of each cookie in the chocolate, let

the excess drip over the pot, and place on a wire

rack set on an aluminum-foil-lined baking sheet to

harden.

Deluxe Four-Layer Bars

I have fond memories of Seven-Layer Bars, a decadently rich confection that was a bake-sale perennial where I grew up. Here's my version, edited down to 4 favorite ingredients plus the secret stuff that holds it all together, sweetened condensed milk. I find that these bars hold together best when chilled slightly before cutting. Put them in the refrigerator for 20 minutes or so, and they won't crumble when lifted from the pan.

MAKES 9 BARS

EQUIPMENT

Measuring cups and measuring spoons

8-inch square baking pan

Food processor fitted with metal blade or large chef's knife

Small bowl

Large spoon

Wire rack

Paring knife

INGREDIENTS

¼ cup (½ stick) unsalted butter, cut into 3 or 4 pieces

1 cup almonds

½ cup dried apricots

¾ cup graham cracker crumbs

½ cup semisweet chocolate chips

1½ cups sweetened flaked coconut

One 7-ounce can sweetened condensed milk

1. Preheat the oven to 325 degrees. Place the butter in the baking pan and place the pan in the oven.

2. Finely chop the almonds in the work bowl of the food processor or by hand. Set aside in the bowl. Coarsely chop the apricots in the food processor or by hand. Stir together with the almonds.

3. Remove the baking pan from the oven, tilt to distribute the butter, and sprinkle the graham cracker crumbs evenly across the bottom of the pan. Sprinkle the almond-and-apricots mixture

over the crumbs. Sprinkle the chocolate chips over the almonds and apricots. Sprinkle the coconut over the chocolate chips. With the spoon, press down on the coconut firmly to pack together the layers. Drizzle the condensed milk evenly over the coconut.

4. Bake until the coconut begins to color, 25 to 27 minutes. Let the pan cool completely on the wire rack. Refrigerate until chilled, for easy cutting. Cut into 9 bars.

◆

Nut Butter Blondies

I love to transform humdrum recipes with the addition or substitution of 1 ingredient. Here, I use hazelnut butter in place of plain old peanut butter to make truly unusual and delicious bar cookies. I'm especially pleased with the result, since hazelnuts themselves are difficult to use in quick desserts because they take so long to skin. Hazelnut butter, as well as almond and cashew butters, is sold in natural foods stores and many supermarkets.

MAKES 9 BARS

EQUIPMENT

Measuring cups and measuring spoons

8-inch square baking pan

Nonstick cooking spray

Large bowl

Electric mixer fitted with paddle attachment

Rubber spatula

Toothpick

Wire rack

Paring knife

INGREDIENTS

6 tablespoons (¾ stick) unsalted butter, softened

½ cup sugar

⅔ cup hazelnut, almond, or cashew butter

2 large eggs

1 teaspoon pure vanilla extract

1 cup plus 2 tablespoons all-purpose flour

½ teaspoon baking powder

¼ teaspoon salt

½ cup semisweet chocolate chips

1. Preheat the oven to 350 degrees. Spray the baking pan with cooking spray.

2. In the bowl, beat together the butter, sugar, and nut butter with the mixer on medium-high speed until well combined. Add the eggs and vanilla and beat, scraping down the sides of the bowl once or twice with the spatula, until well combined. Mix in the flour, baking powder, and salt with the spatula until just combined. Stir in the chocolate chips.

3. Scrape the batter into the prepared pan and smooth with the spatula. Bake until golden and the toothpick inserted into the center of the pan comes out clean, 20 to 25 minutes. Let the pan cool completely on the wire rack, then cut into 9 bars.

◆

Sweet and Spicy Pecan Brittle

Cayenne pepper gives plain pecan praline an interesting kick. Unsalted peanuts make a delicious substitute for pecans.

When melting and caramelizing sugar, my advice is not to stir. Stirring encourages sugar crystals to form on the side of the pan, preventing your caramel from becoming smooth. Just pour the sugar and water into the pan, tilt it a little to moisten the sugar, and let it sit on top of the flame. A greased spoon and spatula will help you work with the hot candy, without having it stick.

MAKES ABOUT ¾ POUND

EQUIPMENT

Measuring cups and measuring spoons
8-inch square baking pan
Heavy-duty aluminum foil
Wooden spoon
Metal spatula
Small saucepan
Chef's knife

INGREDIENTS

Butter for greasing foil, spoon, and spatula
1 cup sugar
¼ cup water
1¼ cups pecans, coarsely chopped
¼ teaspoon cayenne pepper

1. Line the baking pan with aluminum foil and grease the foil with butter. Grease the wooden spoon and spatula with butter also. Combine the sugar and water in the saucepan. Bring to a boil and let boil—without stirring—until the mixture turns a light amber color, 5 to 7 minutes. If parts of the syrup are turning darker than others, gently tilt the pan to even out the cooking.

2. As soon as the syrup is a uniformly amber color, stir in the pecans and cayenne with the greased spoon. Pour the mixture into the prepared pan and smooth with the buttered spatula. Work quickly because the caramel will begin to harden soon after it is removed from

the heat. Allow the mixture to cool completely. When hardened, turn the praline out of the pan, remove the foil, and chop into small chunks with the chef's knife. Praline will keep at room temperature in an airtight container for several weeks.

◆

Honey and Almond Brittle

This brittle is even easier to make than caramel candy made with sugar.
It cooks more quickly (5 minutes or less) and the honey is less temperamental
than the sugar, resulting in glossy, smooth candy every time. Honey and
Almond Brittle is chewy, rather than crunchy—the kind of candy
people happily risk their fillings to enjoy.

MAKES ABOUT ¾ POUND

EQUIPMENT

Measuring cups and measuring spoons
8-inch square baking pan
Heavy-duty aluminum foil
Wooden spoon
Metal spatula
Small saucepan
Chef's knife

INGREDIENTS

Butter for greasing foil, spoon, and spatula
½ cup honey
1 cup whole almonds
1 teaspoon salt

1. Line the baking pan with aluminum foil and grease the foil with butter. Grease the wooden spoon and spatula with butter. Place the honey, almonds, and salt in the saucepan and bring to a boil. Cook over medium-high heat, stirring constantly with the buttered spoon, until the honey is golden brown, 3 to 5 minutes.

2. Pour the mixture into the prepared pan and smooth with the buttered spatula. Allow the mixture to cool completely. When hardened, turn the candy out of the pan, remove the foil, and chop into small chunks with the chef's knife. This brittle will keep at room temperature in an airtight container for several weeks.

Homemade Granola Bars

These wholesome bar cookies have a homemade flavor and texture that you'll never find in a commercially produced granola bar. Any nuts and dried fruits may be substituted for the raisins and walnuts—dried cherries and almonds are another good combination, as are chopped dried figs and pecans.

MAKES 6 BARS

EQUIPMENT

Measuring cups and measuring spoons

8-inch square baking pan

Nonstick cooking spray

Large bowl

Electric mixer fitted with paddle attachment

Rubber spatula

Wire rack

INGREDIENTS

1 large egg

½ cup firmly packed light brown sugar

1 tablespoon vegetable oil

½ teaspoon ground cinnamon

½ teaspoon pure vanilla extract

Pinch of salt

¾ cup rolled (old-fashioned) oats

2 tablespoons all-purpose flour

½ cup golden raisins

¼ cup chopped walnuts

1. Preheat the oven to 325 degrees. Spray the baking pan with cooking spray.

2. Combine the egg, brown sugar, vegetable oil, cinnamon, vanilla, and salt in the bowl with the mixer on medium-low speed. Add the oats, flour, raisins, and walnuts and mix together with the spatula until the batter is evenly moistened.

3. Scrape the batter into the prepared pan and spread evenly along the bottom with the spatula. Bake until golden, about 30 minutes. Let the pan cool completely on the wire rack. Cut into 6 bars.

White Chocolate–Mint Truffles

Use a top-quality brand chocolate rich in cocoa butter (Lindt is widely available).
Make sure to chop the chocolate very fine before adding the boiling cream to
ensure that it all melts, and your truffles will be smooth, not lumpy.

MAKES ABOUT 24 TRUFFLES

EQUIPMENT

Measuring cups and measuring spoons
Chef's knife
Cutting board
Large bowl
Small saucepan
Wire whisk
Shallow bowl

INGREDIENTS

12 ounces high-quality white chocolate
¼ cup (½ stick) unsalted butter
6 tablespoons heavy cream
½ teaspoon pure mint extract
¼ cup unsweetened cocoa powder

1. Finely chop the white chocolate. Place in the large bowl.

2. Heat the butter and heavy cream in the saucepan over medium heat until just boiling. Whisk this into the chocolate and continue to whisk until smooth. Whisk in the mint extract. Refrigerate until set, about 1 hour.

3. Place the cocoa powder in the shallow bowl. One at a time, measure out the truffle mixture in rounded teaspoonfuls. With your palms, quickly roll each truffle into a ball and place in the bowl with the cocoa powder. Turn the truffle to coat. Store the truffles in an airtight container in the refrigerator until serving, up to 3 days.

TRUFFLES

Dark chocolate and milk chocolate truffles become a 15-minute dessert when made in small batches and rolled in cocoa powder or chopped nuts rather than dipped in tempered chocolate. The formula is simple (and slightly different from the formula for white chocolate truffles): Bring ¾ cup heavy cream to a boil. Pour over ¾ pound finely chopped bittersweet or milk chocolate and 2 tablespoons unsalted butter in a bowl and whisk until smooth. Stir in 3 tablespoons liquor or liqueur of your choice, or a small amount of another flavoring, and let cool until set. Roll rounded teaspoonfuls into balls and roll in unsweetened cocoa powder or chopped nuts. Try the following combinations or experiment with others of your own devising.

◆

- ◆ Milk chocolate, raspberry liqueur, and unsweetened cocoa powder
- ◆ Milk chocolate, hazelnut liqueur, and finely chopped skinned hazelnuts
- ◆ Milk chocolate, bourbon, and finely chopped pecans
- ◆ Milk chocolate, ¼ teaspoon pure maple extract, and finely chopped walnuts
- ◆ Bittersweet chocolate, orange liqueur, and unsweetened cocoa powder
- ◆ Bittersweet chocolate, brandy, and unsweetened cocoa powder
- ◆ Bittersweet chocolate, almond liqueur, and finely chopped almonds
- ◆ Bittersweet chocolate, rum, and finely chopped walnuts
- ◆ Bittersweet chocolate, 1 teaspoon instant espresso powder, and finely chopped blanched almonds

Macadamia Nut Fudge

Traditional fudge, made with sugar and half-and-half, cooks on top of the stove over low heat for more than an hour until it reaches 234 degrees on a candy thermometer. It must be carefully cooled on a marble slab before it is transferred to a pan to harden. Quick fudge, made with sweetened condensed milk, takes minutes and doesn't require any special equipment. Most important, it satisfies the most serious chocolate craving just as well. I like to use unusual nuts to make my quick fudge a little bit special. Look for unsalted macadamia nuts in your natural foods store or the natural foods aisle of your supermarket. Other nuts may be substituted, if you like.

MAKES 16 SQUARES

EQUIPMENT

Measuring cups and measuring spoons

Double boiler or medium-size saucepan and medium-size stainless steel bowl

8-inch square baking pan

Chef's knife

Cutting board

Wire whisk

Rubber spatula

INGREDIENTS

Butter for greasing the pan

1 pound bittersweet chocolate

1 cup sweetened condensed milk

1 tablespoon pure vanilla extract

2 cups unsalted macadamia nuts

1. Put 1 inch of water into the bottom of the double boiler or in the saucepan and bring to a bare simmer. Butter the baking pan. Coarsely chop the chocolate. Combine the chocolate and condensed milk in the top of the double boiler or in the steel bowl and set it on top of the simmering water, making sure that the water doesn't touch the bowl. Heat, whisking occasionally, until the chocolate is completely melted.

2. Stir in the vanilla and nuts. Scrape the mixture into the prepared pan and smooth with the spatula. Let the fudge harden (at least 2 hours) then cut into 16 squares. The fudge will keep for several days in an airtight container at room temperature.

INSTANT GRATIFICATION FOR COMPANY

SPECIAL DESSERTS IN THE BLINK OF AN EYE

ORANGE-CARAMEL PARFAITS

BLACKBERRIES WITH CHAMPAGNE SABAYON

FROZEN LEMON SABAYON TERRINE WITH KIWIS AND RASPBERRIES

PARMESAN SHORTBREADS WITH RED WINE STRAWBERRIES

ROASTED GRAPES WITH SOFT-RIPENED BLUE CHEESE

ROASTED FIGS WITH RICOTTA AND HONEY

RUM-CARAMEL FONDUE WITH TROPICAL FRUIT

APRICOT SOUFFLÉS

CHOCOLATE "CREPES" WITH KAHLÚA CREAM

ORANGE MARMALADE "CREPES" WITH WARM STRAWBERRIES AND SOUR CREAM

PUFF PASTRY ICE CREAM SANDWICHES

CHERRY-ALMOND FRANGIPANE TARTS

CHOCOLATE-BOURBON TARTS

S'MORES SUNDAES

B ECAUSE MOST OF THE ENTERTAINING I DO IS STRICTLY casual, I usually have no problem serving Spiced Mexican Chocolate Pudding or Warm Gingerbread Squares to guests. Really good homemade food is a treat in itself, and most people are thrilled to get an exemplary version of an everyday dessert. Sometimes, however, it's nice to serve something a little out of the ordinary, especially if you are celebrating a birthday or anniversary, or just enjoying an evening with grown-ups where you can indulge your adult whims and tastes. Here is the place to look if you want to surprise your guests with something a little bit different.

The following desserts are an eclectic group, chosen for a variety of reasons. Liqueurs and wines grant sophistication to even the most casual preparations. A case in point is Blackberries with Champagne Sabayon. Precious ingredients elevate this variation on berries and cream to entertaining heights.

Desserts combining fruit and cheese are another option. Neither Parmesan Shortbreads with Red Wine Strawberries nor Roasted Grapes with Soft-Ripened Blue Cheese is fancy or difficult to make. But because they resemble a cheese course, in addition to serving as

dessert, they are sure to make your guests feel pampered.

Exotic or unusual fruits also make special desserts. A warm rum-caramel dip for sliced starfruit turns dessert into an event. It's not every day, after all, that you pull out the fondue pot. And the presence of starfruit is itself an event for many people who have never tried it.

Sometimes presentation itself makes desserts special for entertaining. High-rising Apricot Soufflés, although they take less than 15 minutes to prepare, end the meal with a flourish. Similarly impressive are crepes and individual tarts (both made very easy here), which your guests are more likely to see at restaurants and bakeries than at home.

There *are* times that you want to please both parents and kids, or just please the grown-up kid in yourself. Reserve S'mores Sundaes for these occasions. Entertaining can also be an excuse for enjoying a gooey kiddie treat like these whole-wheat blondies topped with dark chocolate ice cream and toasted marshmallows.

Other Entertaining Desserts:

Orange-Caramel Parfaits

Dulce de Leche, the sensational caramel-vanilla flavor from Häagen-Dazs, is great for parfaits, since it is laced with so much rich caramel that no sauce is needed. Simply place a tablespoonful of Grand Marnier at the bottom of each parfait glass, layer with ice cream and nuts, and top with whipped cream for a fun but surprisingly adult frozen dessert.

MAKES 4 SERVINGS

EQUIPMENT

Measuring cups and measuring spoons
Chef's knife
Cutting board
4 parfait glasses or dessert goblets
Ice cream scoop
Plastic wrap
Medium-size bowl
Electric mixer fitted with whisk attachment

INGREDIENTS

½ cup pecans
¼ cup Grand Marnier or other orange liqueur
1 pint Dulce de Leche or other caramel ice cream,
    softened a bit
½ cup heavy cream
2 teaspoons confectioners' sugar

1. Finely chop the pecans. Place 1 tablespoon of the Grand Marnier in each of the parfait glasses or dessert goblets. Place a small scoop of ice cream (about 2 tablespoons) in each glass, sprinkle with ½ tablespoon of the pecans, and press the ice cream into the glass with the back of the scoop so that the liqueur rises over the ice cream. Repeat with 3 more scoops of ice cream and 3 portions of nuts. Cover each glass or goblet with plastic wrap and place in the freezer at least 1 hour or until ready to serve, up to 24 hours.

2. Remove the parfaits from the freezer and let stand for 5 minutes. Place the heavy cream and confectioners' sugar in the bowl and beat on medium-high speed with the mixer until the mixture holds stiff peaks. Top each parfait with some whipped cream and serve.

Blackberries with Champagne Sabayon

If you're serving champagne as an aperitif, reserve a little bit for this simple but festive dessert. To me, blackberries are the most precious variety, most appropriate for entertaining, but raspberries, strawberries, blueberries, or a combination are fine, too.

MAKES 4 SERVINGS

EQUIPMENT
Measuring cups and measuring spoons
Double boiler or medium-size saucepan and
  medium-size stainless steel bowl
Wire whisk
Spoon
4 dessert bowls

INGREDIENTS
3 large egg yolks
1/3 cup plus 2 tablespoons sugar
1/2 cup champagne or sparkling wine
1 pint fresh blackberries

1. Put 1 inch of water into the bottom of the double boiler or in the saucepan and bring to a bare simmer. Whisk the egg yolks and sugar together in the top of the double boiler or in the steel bowl until foamy. Set over the simmering water without letting it touch the water. Whisk constantly, until the mixture begins to thicken, about 1 minute.

2. Slowly whisk in the champagne and continue to cook, whisking constantly, until the mixture is warm to the touch, pale yellow, and about triple in volume, 5 to 7 minutes.

3. Spoon some of the berries into each of the dessert bowls. Spoon the warm sabayon over the berries and serve immediately.

Note: Uncooked eggs should not be used in food to be consumed by children, pregnant women, or anyone in poor health or with a compromised immune system.

Frozen Lemon Sabayon Terrine with Kiwis and Raspberries

Here, I stir some whipped cream into lemon sabayon and freeze the mixture in a loaf pan. The frozen slices look and taste great with a scattering of berries and kiwis.

MAKES 8 SERVINGS

EQUIPMENT

Measuring cups and measuring spoons

Citrus zester

8 x 4-inch loaf pan

Plastic wrap

Double boiler or medium-size saucepan and
    medium-size stainless steel bowl

Wire whisk

Large bowl

Electric mixer fitted with whisk attachment

Rubber spatula

Cutting board

Paring knife

Large plate

Knife

Spoon

8 dessert plates

INGREDIENTS

6 large egg yolks

⅔ cup plus 1 tablespoon sugar

½ cup water

1 teaspoon grated lemon zest

6 tablespoons fresh lemon juice

1 cup heavy cream

3 kiwis

½ pint fresh raspberries

1. Line the loaf pan with plastic wrap, making sure that the wrap is tucked into all the corners and that there is at least 1 inch overhanging the top of the pan on all sides.

2. Put 1 inch of water into the bottom of the double boiler or saucepan and bring to a bare simmer. Whisk the yolks and ⅔ cup of the sugar in the top of the double boiler or in the steel bowl until foamy. Set the bowl over

the water. Whisk constantly, until the mixture begins to thicken, about 1 minute.

3. Slowly whisk in the water, zest, and juice and continue to cook, whisking constantly, until the mixture is warm to the touch, pale yellow, and about triple in volume, about 5 minutes. Set aside to let cool to room temperature.

4. Place the heavy cream and remaining 1 tablespoon sugar into the bowl and beat with the mixer on medium-high speed until it holds stiff peaks. Gently fold the whipped cream into the cooled sabayon with the spatula, being careful not to deflate the cream. Gently scrape the mixture into the loaf pan and smooth the top with the spatula. Cover the top with plastic wrap and refrigerate until firm, at least 6 hours and up to 24 hours.

5. To serve, peel the kiwis with the paring knife and cut into thin rounds. Remove the sabayon from the freezer and gently tug the plastic wrap that lines the pan to loosen it. Place the plate over the pan and turn it over. Gently tap to release. Peel the plastic wrap away from the sabayon and cut into slices with a sharp knife. Place each slice on a dessert plate, spoon some kiwis and berries around each slice, and serve immediately.

Parmesan Shortbreads with Red Wine Strawberries

Savory Parmesan cookies provide just the right balance for strawberries
marinated in red wine. Parmesan shortbreads may also be served
on their own as appetizers.

MAKES 4 SERVINGS

EQUIPMENT

Measuring cups and measuring spoons

Paring knife

Food processor fitted with metal blade

Rolling pin

5-inch saucer

Baking sheet

Wire rack

Small bowl

Cutting board

Spoon

4 dessert bowls

INGREDIENTS

¼ cup (½ stick) cold unsalted butter

1 cup freshly grated Parmesan cheese

½ cup all-purpose flour

2 tablespoons sugar

¼ cup dry red wine

1 pint fresh strawberries

1. Preheat the oven to **425** degrees. Cut the
butter into 6 or 8 pieces. Place the butter and
cheese in the work bowl of the food processor
and pulse several times until the mixture
resembles coarse meal. Add the flour and
process until the dough comes together in a
ball, about 1 minute. Divide the dough in half
and shape into 2 disks.

2. Roll each disk into a 5¼-inch round. Place the
saucer upside down on top of each disk and trim
the dough around the edge to create an even
circle. Cut each circle into 8 wedges. Place the
wedges ½ inch apart on the baking sheet and
bake until lightly browned, 5 to 7 minutes.
Remove the shortbreads to cool on the wire rack.

3. While the biscuits are baking, combine the sugar and wine in the small bowl. Stir to dissolve the sugar. Slice the tops off the berries and cut each berry in half. Add the berries to the wine, tossing to coat and let stand until ready to serve.

4. Divide the berries and wine among the dessert bowls. Tuck 2 shortbreads into each of the bowls, and serve the additional shortbreads on the side.

Roasted Grapes with Soft-Ripened Blue Cheese

I've tried these grapes with sharp cheeses like Roquefort and Maytag Blue, but in the end I prefer a smooth cheese that provides a creamy contrast. If you are a real fan of sharp blue cheeses, however, serve the roasted grapes with your favorite.

MAKES 4 SERVINGS

EQUIPMENT
Measuring cups and measuring spoons
Shallow 8-inch square baking dish
Paring knife
Spoon
4 dessert bowls

INGREDIENTS
¼ cup sugar
3 tablespoons water
1 vanilla bean, split
3 cups seedless red grapes, stemmed
4 ounces Gorgonzola Dolce, Blue Castello, or other mild, creamy blue cheese

1. Preheat the oven to 425 degrees. Combine the sugar, water, and vanilla bean in the baking dish; stir to dissolve the sugar. Add the grapes to the dish and bake for 15 minutes, shaking once or twice. Discard the vanilla bean.

2. Divide the grapes among the dessert bowls; drizzle the syrup from the baking dish over the grapes. Slice the cheese into 8 thin strips and place 2 strips in an X on top of each portion of grapes.

Roasted Figs with Ricotta and Honey

I keep bowls of grapes, bunches of bananas, and chunks of watermelon around for everyday desserts, but for some reason I always save fresh figs for company. This quick dessert would make a spectacular ending to a rustic Italian meal— pasta with fresh tomato sauce, grilled veal chops, and a green salad.

MAKES 4 SERVINGS

EQUIPMENT
Measuring cups and measuring spoons
Paring knife
Baking sheet
4 dessert plates

INGREDIENTS
8 ripe fresh figs
1 tablespoon sugar
1 tablespoon unsalted butter
1⅓ cups whole-milk ricotta cheese
2 tablespoons honey

1. Position an oven rack as close to the heating element as possible and preheat the broiler. Stem and halve the figs lengthwise. Place them on the baking sheet cut side up and sprinkle with the sugar. Cut the butter into very small pieces and dot the figs with them. Place the figs as close to the heat as possible and broil until they begin to brown around the edges, about 2 minutes.

2. Place ⅓ cup of the ricotta on each of the dessert plates. Drizzle each with ½ tablespoon of the honey. Arrange the warm figs alongside each portion of ricotta and serve immediately.

Rum-Caramel Fondue
with Tropical Fruit

Part of the craze for all things retro, fondue has made a comeback in the past few years. So, unearth that old fondue pot, or unpack the new one you got last Christmas, and entertain your friends with this simple but special recipe. Other fruits can be used instead; strawberries and peach slices aren't tropical, but they are delicious when dipped in this rich, warm sauce. If you don't have a fondue pot, warm 4 small ramekins in a preheated 200-degree oven for 10 minutes and pour a little sauce into each one right before serving. The caramel should stay warm this way long enough for your guests to devour it.

MAKES 4 SERVINGS

EQUIPMENT

Measuring cups and measuring spoons

Small saucepan

Paring knife

Cutting board

Serving platter

Bamboo skewers for serving

Long-handled wooden spoon

Heatproof serving dish and warming candle for serving

INGREDIENTS

1 cup sugar

¼ cup water

2 ripe but firm bananas

3 starfruit

¾ cup heavy cream

2 tablespoons rum

1. Combine the sugar and ¼ cup water in the saucepan. Bring to a boil and let boil until the mixture turns a light amber color, 5 to 7 minutes. Do not stir. If parts of the syrup are

turning darker than others, gently tilt the pan to even out the cooking.

2. Prepare the fruit while the caramel is cooking, but keep a close eye on it so it doesn't burn. Peel the bananas and slice into ¾-inch chunks. For the starfruit, use the paring knife to peel off the hard ridges on the top of the five ribs. The remaining peel is edible. Slice the fruit crosswise into ¼-inch-thick starshapes. Arrange the fruit on the platter with the bamboo skewers.

3. As soon as the syrup is a uniformly amber color, remove the pan from the heat. At arm's length, pour the heavy cream into the pot. Stir with the wooden spoon until combined. Be careful; the cream may splatter. Stir in the rum. (If you haven't finished preparing the fruit, do so now.)

4. Place the sauce in a heatproof serving dish over a warming candle. Serve warm with the fruit.

◆

Apricot Soufflés

These egg white soufflés get an incredibly high rise. Run the jam through
the food processor to liquefy—it needs to be very smooth before
it can be incorporated into the whipped egg whites.

MAKES 4 SERVINGS

EQUIPMENT

Measuring cups and measuring spoons
Four 10-ounce ramekins
Nonstick cooking spray
Food processor fitted with metal blade
Large bowl
Electric mixer fitted with whisk attachment
Rubber spatula
Small fine-mesh strainer

INGREDIENTS

2 tablespoons plus 2 teaspoons granulated sugar
1 cup best-quality apricot jam
4 large egg whites
Confectioners' sugar for dusting

1. Preheat the oven to 400 degrees. Spray the ramekins evenly with cooking spray and sprinkle each with ½ teaspoon of the granulated sugar, coating the bottom and sides.

2. Place the jam in the work bowl of the food processor and process until smooth.

3. Place the egg whites in the bowl and beat on low speed with the mixer until frothy. Turn to high and beat, adding the remaining 2 tablespoons granulated sugar in a slow stream, until the mixture holds soft peaks. Gently fold the jam into the egg whites with the spatula.

4. Divide the mixture among the prepared ramekins and bake until risen and lightly browned, 12 to 14 minutes. Dust with confectioners' sugar using the strainer and serve immediately.

Chocolate "Crepes" with Kahlúa Cream

Egg roll wrappers, sold in the produce section of the supermarket, make a very good substitute for homemade and time-consuming crepes. Filled with chopped chocolate and pan-fried in butter with a little bit of cinnamon and sugar, they get wonderfully crispy. Kahlúa-spiked whipped cream complements the "crepes" in both flavor and texture.

MAKES 4 SERVINGS

EQUIPMENT

Measuring cups and measuring spoons

Large bowl

Electric mixer fitted with whisk attachment

Chef's knife

Cutting board

Small bowl

Large sauté pan

Metal spatula

4 dessert plates

INGREDIENTS

½ cup heavy cream

2 tablespoons sugar

1½ tablespoons Kahlúa

4 ounces bittersweet chocolate

¼ teaspoon ground cinnamon

8 egg roll wrappers

3 tablespoons unsalted butter

1. Place the heavy cream, 1 tablespoon of the sugar, and the Kahlúa in the large bowl and beat with the mixer on high speed until it holds soft peaks.

2. Finely chop the chocolate. Combine the remaining 1 tablespoon sugar and the cinnamon in the small bowl. Place some of the chocolate in a ½-inch-thick line across the bottom quarter of each egg roll wrapper. Roll up tightly.

(continued)

3. Melt the butter in the sauté pan over medium heat. Carefully add the "crepes" (once they crisp up, they won't unroll) and sprinkle with the cinnamon sugar. Cook until golden brown on the bottom, 1 to 2 minutes. Turn with the spatula and cook until golden brown on the other side, about 1 minute.

4. With the spatula, Place 2 "crepes" on each of the dessert plates. Garnish with the whipped cream and serve immediately.

Orange Marmalade "Crepes" with Warm Strawberries and Sour Cream

This is a very pretty dish, and one of the most delicious and satisfying recipes that I developed for this book. Sliced strawberries briefly cooked in Grand Marnier make a perfect finish for the crispy "crepes." The sweetness of the hot marmalade filling is balanced by a garnish of tangy sour cream.

MAKES 4 SERVINGS

EQUIPMENT

Measuring cups and measuring spoons
Cutting board
Paring knife
Large sauté pan
Metal spatula
Spoon
4 dessert plates

INGREDIENTS

1 pint fresh strawberries
½ cup orange marmalade
8 egg roll wrappers
3 tablespoons unsalted butter
1 tablespoon sugar
¼ cup Grand Marnier or other orange liqueur
½ cup sour cream

1. Slice the tops off the strawberries and slice thin. Set aside.

2. Place 1 tablespoon of the marmalade in a ½-inch-thick line across the bottom quarter of each egg roll wrapper. Roll up tightly.

3. Heat the butter in the sauté pan over medium heat. Carefully add the "crepes" (once they crisp up, they won't unroll) and sprinkle with the sugar. Cook until golden brown on the bottom, 1 to 2 minutes. Turn with the spatula and cook until golden brown on the other side, about 1 minute.

4. Using the spatula, place 2 "crepes" on each plate. Add the strawberries and Grand Marnier

to the pan, turn the heat up to medium-high,
and cook until the alcohol aroma has dissipated,
1 to 2 minutes. Spoon some of the berries over
each serving, top each with a dollop of sour
cream, and serve immediately.

Puff Pastry Ice Cream Sandwiches

Here is a terrific use for store-bought puff pastry and a convenient way to dress up ice cream for company. You can cut the pastry circles well in advance, make the sauce several hours ahead of time, and bake the pastry just before serving so that it provides a warm contrast to the ice cream.

MAKES 4 SERVINGS

EQUIPMENT

Measuring spoons

Paring knife

Food processor fitted with metal blade

Rubber spatula

Baking sheet

Fork

Small bowl

Pastry brush

Wire rack

4 dessert plates

INGREDIENTS

1 sheet (about ½ pound) frozen puff pastry, thawed

½ pint fresh strawberries

1½ teaspoons confectioners' sugar

1 large egg

1 teaspoon granulated sugar

1 pint vanilla or mint chocolate chip ice cream, softened a bit

1. Preheat the oven to 425 degrees.

2. Unfold the puff pastry and, using the top of the ice cream container as a template if you like, cut four 4-inch circles with the paring knife. Freeze for at least 15 minutes or cover with plastic wrap and freeze for up to 2 weeks.

3. Cut the tops off the berries and place the berries in the work bowl of the food processor. Add the confectioners' sugar and process, scraping down the sides of the bowl once or twice as necessary with the spatula, until

smooth. (The strawberry sauce may be made several hours in advance, covered, and refrigerated. Stir before using.)

4. Transfer the pastry circles to the baking sheet. Lightly beat the egg in the bowl, then lightly brush the pastry circles with the egg (too much egg will weigh down the pastry and prevent it from fully puffing) and sprinkle with the granulated sugar. Bake until puffed and golden brown, 15 to 17 minutes. Transfer the baking sheet to the wire rack. Let cool for several minutes.

5. Place each warm puff pastry circle on a plate and split it with the paring knife. Place a scoop of ice cream on the bottom portion of each circle. Spoon some sauce over the ice cream. Top with the upper portion of the circle and serve immediately.

◆

Cherry-Almond Frangipane Tarts

Individual tarts look so perfect and professional that they are like little presents at the end of a meal. Usually, though, they are too labor-intensive to make in just a few minutes. By streamlining a recipe for a favorite nut-and-fruit tart, I've been able to get these gems in the oven in less than 15 minutes. Frangipane is a rich nut batter that's usually used as a filling. Here, I use it on its own, without rolled pastry dough. Dried cherries added to the batter obviate the need for fruit on top. A scoop of ice cream finishes off the dessert. If you like, you can make the batter several hours ahead of time and refrigerate until just before dinner. Bake the tarts just before you sit down to eat, and serve them warm a few minutes after they come out of the oven.

MAKES 4 TARTS

EQUIPMENT

Measuring cups and measuring spoons

Butter knife

Four 4-inch tart pans with removable bottoms or one
    8-inch tart pan

Nonstick cooking spray

Food processor fitted with metal blade

Rubber spatula

Small fine-mesh strainer

4 dessert plates

INGREDIENTS

1½ cups (about 6 ounces) blanched almonds

½ cup granulated sugar

2 large eggs

½ teaspoon pure almond extract

2 tablespoons unsalted butter

2 tablespoons all-purpose flour

¼ teaspoon baking powder

1 cup dried cherries

Confectioners' sugar for dusting

½ pint vanilla ice cream, softened a bit

1. Preheat the oven to 375 degrees. Spray the tart pans with cooking spray.

2. Combine the almonds and granulated sugar in the work bowl of the food processor and process until the almonds are finely ground. Add the eggs and almond extract and pulse several times to combine. Cut the butter into 6 pieces, add to the work bowl, and pulse several times to combine. Add the flour and baking powder and pulse once or twice to combine. Add the cherries and pulse once to combine.

3. Scrape the batter evenly into the prepared tart pans and smooth the top with the spatula. Bake until slightly puffed and golden, 20 to 25 minutes (30 to 35 minutes for 1 large tart). Remove from the oven and let cool for 5 to 10 minutes. Remove the tarts from the pans and place on the plates. Sprinkle with confectioners' sugar using the strainer. Serve warm with ice cream on the side.

Chocolate-Bourbon Tarts

This dessert combines the flavors found in Mississippi mud cake—chocolate, bourbon, and coffee. If you are not a bourbon fan, you can substitute something else. Grand Marnier and dark rum are good with vanilla ice cream; crème de menthe is good with vanilla or mint chocolate chip.

MAKES 4 TARTS

EQUIPMENT

Measuring cups and measuring spoons
Four 4-inch tart pans with removable bottoms or one
    8-inch tart pan
Nonstick cooking spray
Double boiler or medium-size saucepan and
    medium-size stainless steel bowl
Chef's knife
Cutting board
Wire whisk
Large bowl
Rubber spatula
Electric mixer fitted with paddle attachment
Wire rack
Pastry brush
Metal spatula
4 dessert plates

INGREDIENTS

2½ ounces unsweetened chocolate
2 tablespoons unsalted butter
1 cup sugar
½ teaspoon pure vanilla extract
6 tablespoons bourbon
2 large eggs
½ cup all-purpose flour
½ pint coffee ice cream, softened a bit

1. Preheat the oven to 350 degrees. Spray the tart pans with cooking spray.

2. Put 1 inch of water in the bottom of the double boiler or in the saucepan and bring to a bare simmer. Finely chop the chocolate. Combine the chocolate and butter in the top of the double boiler or in the steel bowl and set on top of the simmering water, making sure that

the water doesn't touch the bowl. Heat, whisking occasionally, until completely melted.

3. Scrape the chocolate mixture into the bowl, using the spatula. Add the sugar, vanilla, and 3 tablespoons of the bourbon and mix on low speed with the mixer to combine. With the mixer on low speed, add the eggs, one at a time, scraping down the sides of the bowl after each addition with the spatula. Add the flour and mix with the spatula to combine.

4. Scrape the batter evenly into the prepared tart pans and smooth the top with the spatula. Bake until just firm to the touch in the center, 20 to 25 minutes (30 to 35 minutes for a large tart). Remove the tarts from the oven, transfer to the wire rack, and brush with the remaining 2 tablespoons bourbon. Let cool for 5 to 10 minutes, remove from the pans and transfer to the plates. Serve warm with the ice cream on the side.

◆

S'mores Sundaes

Here's a dessert I choose when entertaining my friends and their children. Kids love the gooey marshmallow topping, but it's really just an excuse for all of us parents to enjoy toasted marshmallows. Blondies made with whole-wheat flour are a nod to the graham crackers in S'mores. Wholesome and chewy, they contrast nicely with the rest of the gooey ingredients in the dessert.

MAKES 8 SERVINGS

EQUIPMENT

Measuring cups and measuring spoons

8-inch square baking pan

Nonstick cooking spray

Butter warmer or small saucepan

Wooden spoon

Large bowl

Rubber spatula

Toothpick

Wire rack

Paring knife

8 large sundae dishes

4 metal skewers

INGREDIENTS

½ cup (1 stick) unsalted butter

1 large egg

1 teaspoon pure vanilla extract

1 cup whole-wheat flour

1 cup firmly packed light brown sugar

1 teaspoon baking powder

⅛ teaspoon salt

¾ cup chopped walnuts

8 or more marshmallows

1½ pints chocolate ice cream, softened a bit

1. Preheat the oven to 350 degrees. Spray the baking pan with cooking spray. Melt the butter in the butter warmer or saucepan.

2. Stir together the butter, egg, and vanilla in the bowl. Stir in the flour, brown sugar, baking powder, and salt until combined. Stir in the walnuts. Scrape the mixture into the prepared pan and smooth the top with the spatula. Bake until golden and the toothpick inserted into the

center comes out clean, 20 to 23 minutes. Let the pan cool on the wire rack. Cut into 16 squares.

3. Place 2 blondies in each of the sundae dishes. Thread 2 marshmallows on each of the skewers and toast over an open flame (either a grill or a gas burner on a cooktop will do) until soft and golden brown. Top the blondies with a scoop of ice cream and top each portion with a toasted marshmallow. Serve immediately.

Owe a bunch of people invitations? If you'd rather bake than barbecue, why not skip dinner and just serve dessert? Here are a few menu ideas to satisfy a variety of tastes and occasions.

✦

FRESH TASTES OF SUMMER

When produce is at its peak and people are really craving light, cool, refreshing desserts, any and all of these are sure to satisfy. Sparkling wine, iced tea, and chilled water with lemon slices are equally refreshing beverages.

Wonton "Canapés" with Crème Fraîche and Diced Mango (page 38)
Blueberry-Maple Semifreddo (page 142)
Almond-Scented Cream Cake (page 104)
Lemon–Cream Cheese Shortbreads (page 172)
Sweet and Spicy Pecan Brittle (page 186)
White Chocolate–Mint Truffles (page 190)

✦

KILLER CHOCOLATE DESSERT PARTY

If your guests can never have too much of a good thing, they'll appreciate the following spread. Strong coffee goes well with any of these desserts, as does ice-cold milk. Serve Homemade Vanilla Wafers (page 176) as a palate cleanser.

Easiest, Best Chocolate Mousse Cake (page 84)
Cocoa Mascarpone and Raspberry Tart with a Chocolate-Almond Crust (page 55)

Deluxe Four-Layer Bars (page 182)
Macadamia Nut Fudge (page 192)
Chocolate "Crepes" with Kahlúa Cream (page 209)

◆

SWEET "HORS D'OEUVRES"
With this menu of "finger foods" you won't need to set the table with plates, forks, or spoons.

Tiny Coconut Macaroons (page 23)
Mini Peanut Butter Cups (page 24)
Maple Walnut Meringues (page 163)
Mocha Shortbread (page 170)
Anise-Flavored Butter Cookies (page 174)
Apricots Stuffed with Almond Paste (page 34)

◆

DESSERT BRUNCH
Play short-order cook and treat some friends to a guilty pleasure—dessert for breakfast. To assuage your guilt, put together a nice fruit salad as an accompaniment.

Pecan Waffles with Rum Raisin Ice Cream (page 30)
Dessert French Toast with Almond Cream (page 32)
Orange Marmalade "Crepes" with Warm Strawberries and Sour Cream (page 211)

◆

ICE CREAM FOUR WAYS

Premium ice cream gets special treatment in the following menu. Make the bananas, pound cake, puff pastry shells, and whole-wheat blondies for the S'mores ahead of time and break out the ice cream as you announce the choices to your guests.

Sautéed Brown Sugar Bananas over Coconut Ice Cream (page 22)
Golden Honey Pound Cake with Chocolate and Vanilla Ice Cream (page 108)
Puff Pastry Ice Cream Sandwiches (page 213)
S'mores Sundaes (page 219)

◆

TART PARTY

Show off the versatility of this dessert form with a few stellar examples. All of the tarts are do-ahead, so you'll be able to enjoy your own party.

Quickest Pecan Tart (page 48)
Blueberry-Coconut Tart (page 59)
White Chocolate–Mint Tart with Strawberries (page 57)
Cherry-Almond Frangipane Tarts (page 215)
Chocolate-Bourbon Tarts (page 217)

◆

Index